PRAISE FOR CA

"*Fierce with Age* is thought-provoking, brave, and courageous. Carol Orsborn tackles both the shadow and promise of transitioning beyond midlife, showing us aging as the opportunity to grow whole, rather than just grow old."

—MADDY AND KEN DYCHTWALD, AUTHORS
AND CO-FOUNDERS OF *AGE WAVE*

"In a youth-centric society, Boomer women have understandably resisted the notion of growing old, but there comes a time in every life when denial of aging cracks. This is a time ripe for a book like *Fierce with Age.*"

—MARTI BARLETTA, AUTHOR OF *MARKETING TO WOMEN* AND *PRIMETIME WOMEN*

"In an age where America creates elder ghettos, a brave woman comes out swinging. Her chronicle of a woman's life after 50 is an inspiration for countless other women (and men) to bust through the stereotypes of aging."

—JUSTINE WILLIS TOMS, CO-FOUNDER OF NEW
DIMENSIONS RADIO AND AUTHOR OF *SMALL
PLEASURES: FINDING GRACE IN A CHAOTIC WORLD*

"Through lyrically written pages of her memoir, *Fierce with Age,* Dr. Carol Orsborn conveys today's vital challenge for the Baby Boomer generation: to understand and accept aging and all the ramifications. This book is a poignant invitation for Boomers to try on the liberating possibilities of aging, freed from denial and dodging. Through Orsborn's lucid spiritual lens, coupled with the sophisticated nuances of a Boomer generation marketing expert, readers witness wisdom, wit, and wrath of a well-considered journey. Her memoir shares insightful stories, reflections and advice that can help Boomers discard illusions and illegitimacies of youth obsession, revealing instead the intellectual, emotional, and spiritual paths toward acceptance of the aging process, fiercely."

—BRENT GREEN, AUTHOR OF *MARKETING TO
LEADING-EDGE BABY BOOMERS* AND *GENERATION
REINVENTION*

"Dr. Carol Orsborn confronts aging—not gracefully, but fiercely—inviting us on her journey of unflinching honesty and tender revelation. Her diary of growing older may inspire your own."

> —MARY LOU QUINLAN, AUTHOR OF THE GOD BOX

"By telling us her story of struggle and transformation, Carol gives us hope that we, too, can be 'fierce with age' and, so, live fully with the fire for life."

> —ROBERT L. WEBER, PROFESSOR OF PSYCHOLOGY, HARVARD MEDICAL SCHOOL DEPARTMENT OF PSYCHIATRY

"This is a rich, intimate, and hard-to-put-down read that reminds me aging may not be for sissies, but it can be for seers, adventurers, and a few lucky squirrels. Carol Orsborn takes me there."

> —LEAH KOMAIKO, AUTHOR OF AM I OLD YET?

"Carol Orsborn bravely invites us to accompany her as she wanders in the wilderness of doubt and confusion after her job and identity are stripped away, and as she gradually claims new dreams and renewed faith. Orsborn's searingly honest and ultimately hopeful account of turning toward aging offers invaluable inspiration to all of us who are, or will be, on the journey of later life."

> —RABBI DAYLE A. FRIEDMAN, MSW, MAJCS, BCC, AUTHOR OF JEWISH VISIONS FOR AGING

"I've not read anything as honest and revealing as the tale of Carol Orsborn's personal journey into becoming *Fierce with Age*. Through searching deeply and having the courage to share the experience, she offers us all insights and validation of who we can become in midlife and the years beyond."

> —CONNIE GOLDMAN, AUTHOR OF WHO AM I... NOW THAT I'M NOT WHO I WAS?

"What a ride! With humility, humor and courageous honesty, Carol Orsborn invites us along on her journey from paralyzing fear through surrender to wisdom. What the author shares about facing the unknown and growing to embrace uncertainty will appeal to everyone who worries about losing a job or losing faith."

—PATTI BREITMAN, AUTHOR OF *HOW TO SAY NO WITHOUT FEELING GUILTY*, FOR *THE YEAR I SAVED MY (DOWNSIZED) SOUL*

"A wonderful new book about remembering the most important thing in life—love." —GERALD G. JAMPOLSKY, AUTHOR OF *LOVE IS LETTING GO OF FEAR*, FOR *THE ART OF RESILIENCE*

"One of the cornerstones of building the organization of the future will be distinguishing intrinsic from extrinsic motivation. Orsborn's concept of inner excellence is an excellent place for managers seriously interested in cultivating intrinsic motivation to begin their quest."

—PETER SENGE, AUTHOR OF *THE FIFTH DISCIPLINE*, FOR *INNER EXCELLENCE AT WORK*

"Fresh and funny and spiritual . . . an easily accessible guide for helping us live fuller lives. Supremely useful."

—JOHN NAISBITT, AUTHOR OF *GLOBAL PARADOX*, FOR *HOW WOULD CONFUCIUS ASK FOR A RAISE?*

"I hope many readers will follow Carol Orsborn on her spiritual journey and will learn something about their own souls in the process."

—HAROLD S. KUSHNER, AUTHOR OF *WHEN BAD THINGS HAPPEN TO GOOD PEOPLE*, FOR *RETURN FROM EXILE*

FIERCE
WITH AGE

FIERCE
WITH AGE

CHASING GOD
AND SQUIRRELS
IN BROOKLYN

CAROL ORSBORN

TURNER
PUBLISHING COMPANY

www.turnerpublishing.com

Fierce with Age: Chasing God and Squirrels in Brooklyn

The poem "Quietness" on page 152 is excerpted from *The Essential Rumi,* translated by Coleman Barks, HarperCollins: San Francisco, 1995. Used with permission.

All Scripture passages are excerpted from *The Holy Scriptures,* Jewish Publication Society of America: Philadelphia, 1917.

Cover design: Gina Binkley
Book design: Kym Whitley

Library of Congress Catalog-in-Publishing Data

Orsborn, Carol.
 Fierce with age : chasing God and squirrels in Brooklyn / Carol Orsborn.
  p. cm.
 ISBN 978-1-62045-520-3
 1. Aging--Psychological aspects. I. Title.
 BF724.55.A35O77 2013
 155.67--dc23

                        2012041536

Printed in the United States of America

To Dan

Growing old together is my greatest joy

CONTENTS

CONTENTS

PART TWO: WINTER

Part Three: Spring

PART FOUR: SUMMER

APPENDICES

ACKNOWLEDGMENTS

Revs. Heather Principe and Susan Mufson
The New Seminary School of Interfaith Studies in Manhattan
Diane Caughey, Ph.D., *Stillpoint,*
and Sr. Patricia Beirne, RSM,
The Spirituality Center at Mount St. Mary's College
Leanne Flask
And the Coro Health Executive Team
Robert L. Weber, Ph.D.; Dayle Friedman, MSW, MAJCS,
BCC; Justine Toms, Ph.D.; Mary Ann Brussat,
Frank Mullins, and Claire Altman, JD, MPA
CoroFaith Advisory Board
Agent Linda Roghaar, *whose never-ending talent
and passion for books is truly inspirational*
Publisher Todd Bottorff, Senior Editor Christina Huffines,
Acquisitions Editor Diane Gedymin,
Marketing Executive Lianna McMasters,
Copy Editor Ann Moller,
And the entire visionary publishing team for
Fierce with Age *at Turner Publishing*
H. Rick Moody and Connie Goldman
*And the many spiritual luminaries and authors whose work
inspires the pages of this book*
My family
Dan,
Jody, and
Grant, Ginny, and Grandson Mason

My gratitude to all of you is fierce, indeed!

AUTHOR'S NOTE

Drawn from my diary,
this book is a tell-all about the state of my soul,
not about any particular individuals or companies.
Names and details have been altered
and some characters are composites
inspired by real people,
conversations and events.

Now we are beyond the narcissism of youth,
above the survival struggles of young adulthood,
beyond the grind of middle-age,
and prepared to look beyond ourselves
into the very heartbeat of life.
Now we can let our spirits fly.
We can do what our souls demand
that fully human beings do.
This is the moment for which we were born.

—JOAN CHITTISTER

FIERCE
WITH AGE

INTRODUCTION
WILD SPACE

I DIDN'T KNOW I WAS WRITING A BOOK ABOUT MY journey into the wild space beyond midlife for an entire season of keeping up my daily diary. But then again, when I started this bravest of all my diaries, I was still "Carol Orsborn."

Now, I'm not. I'm something else entirely than the brand and identity that has defined me over the past six decades and twenty books. This is not necessarily a bad thing. In fact, I'm surprisingly re-energized about who I am becoming, and fiercely curious about what lies ahead. As I said, this is not a bad thing—but certainly different. And, may I add, this takes a fair amount of getting used to.

Just one year previously, I had been an accomplished author, scholar, and businesswoman at the peak of my career. After twenty books on spirituality, a doctorate in religion, and recovery from breast cancer years ago, my relationship with God was secure. Basking in the heat of midlife, I prided myself on looking and acting at least ten years younger than my chronological age. As much as I welcomed the birth of my first grandchild, I couldn't believe that I was old enough to have sourced not just one, but two generations. I took comfort in the fact that the average age of grandparents in America is forty-something, so much younger than the stereotypes. While I knew I was not forty (not even as in "sixty is the new forty"), I did think I was going to be, at the very least, "the new sixty."

This ebullient mood, alas, was not to last for long. For reasons you will soon learn, my persona unexpectedly found itself cracked open against the onslaught of time. One moment, I was a smart, spiritual woman at the peak of her game. The next moment, it was as if I had forgotten everything I'd learned over the course of my life. I'd forgotten how to be powerful, how to feel worthy and visible. I'd even forgotten how to pray. Shockingly out of control, I could not get things to go back the way they were, complete a grieving process, or beat a diagnosis. Rather, I had entered no less than a new, prolonged life stage: one that our entire society either denies, reviles, or sentimentalizes in order to trivialize.

In short, I had become old.

As I write this introduction at the end of this year's transition, no one is more surprised, or gratified, than I to have emerged with a most astonishing discovery: that I'm okay with this. In fact, I am more than merely accepting aging. I am actually excited about this new life stage for one very good reason: I am catching my first, promising glimpse of what it truly means to be free. Plummet into aging, stare mortality in the eye, surrender everything, and what else is there left to fear? The way is perilous, danger on all sides. But I am no longer a woman afraid of age. I have become, instead, a woman fierce with age.

My diary had unknowingly begun its journey towards publication most of the way through this tumultuous year, when I bumped into an old friend—or should I say a good friend coming to grips with the fact that in the year since we'd last met, she, too, had grown old. In Celia's case, it had been an illness that turned her from a lithe dance instructor who could not only choreograph the steps but do them, into an elderly woman who needed a walker. I admit I was shocked. She looked much smaller, grayer, and more melancholy. But beneath the veneer of frailty, Celia was still Celia to me.

When she asked what I'd been up to, I shocked her back. I didn't have any glamorous book tour to report. No new client. The fact that I had nothing noteworthy to share was entirely uncharacteristic of me. I struggled to find the words to describe this strange new place in which I'd found myself. Then, from depths unknown, I decided to tell her about the private diary I'd been keeping.

"Frankly, Celia, I've been grappling with the unexpected onset of growing older. One day, it was business as usual. Then suddenly, I found myself feeling ashamed for still being alive."

"It's stupid, isn't it," she nodded in agreement. "The biggest emotion I feel about needing a walker is embarrassment. What the hell is that about?"

"I'm not going to lie," I said. "I had a tough year. In fact, keeping a diary was the only thing that kept me going. Writing it all down, I managed to turn myself from victim to witness. Then life got good again."

"Really?" she said. "And you captured all this in your diary? Can I read it?"

That was the day this book was born. Celia opened up the possibility that speaking my journey towards wholeness out loud might actually be of use to others. But after writing more than twenty books, I also knew that making the commitment to turn my diary into a published book was not one to be undertaken lightly. There would be questions I would have to wrestle with about how much of my own journey I would actually want to make public, particularly given the always vulnerable and often embarrassing nature of so many of my entries. There would also be sensitivities about respecting the intimate details of family members, friends, and peers who did not know that they were to end up as characters in a book. And, too, there would be the tension between telling the story just as it unfolded versus bringing expanded perspective to the writing, editing, and publishing process as I continue making sense of the year just past.

Buoyed by Celia's encouragement, I trust the effort will be worth it. After all, I've already come so far. Not, by any means, as judged by any external criteria. For as I write this introduction at diary's end, I am surrounded by moving boxes that not only symbolize but actually contain the artifacts of midlife marked for storage. And while the movers know the exact storage facility where my lifetime of goods is going, I am none too sure where I, myself, am headed. No matter. Whatever happens with me next, I am feeling unbridled, wild, feral, even. Plus, I have remembered how to pray.

Because of everything I've endured, I begin this new phase of my life journey no longer ashamed or depleted about aging, but rather, curious and excited. While the contours of this wild terrain beyond midlife have not yet fully revealed themselves to me, I am clear that rather than experiencing myself at an ending, I am most definitively starting something profoundly and unexpectedly new. This initiation of a fresh life stage bears with it the hallmarks of all the previous life stages combined: the high anticipation, the celebration, and the bold, outright terror. And so it is that I end this introduction—and this year—fundamentally changed for the good. I would not have it any other way.

FALL

Old age is a plain,
an alto plano,
with nothing when you come
onto it but horizon;
there are few discernible features,
at least at first glance,
no tracks to follow.
Accustomed to limits,
to guidelines,
to markers,
you stand there stunned,
amazed.
You haven't had such a sense of space
since you were twenty—
the splendor, the terror of it.

—Marvin Barrett

1

EPIPHANY

MY JOURNEY TO THE WILD SIDE OF MIDLIFE started in the heart of a mean fall in New York City. One week previously, I had been at the peak of my career, loving my job working for the start-up of my dreams. I was actually being paid fairly by the CEO, who shared my missionary passion for getting brand marketers to take women at midlife seriously. When I'd landed the job several years before, the only woman in her fifties or over on the team, I had taken on the very public role of poster girl for my generation. To attract clients, I blogged and spoke about whatever was on my mind on the company's Web site. To top it off, I truly believed I was doing God's work. Life was sweet.

Happily, for those first few years on the job, what I wanted to write about and what marketers wanted to hear about older women pretty much coincided. I loved to shock young creatives with stories about grandmothers climbing the Himalayas and taking up surfing. I wrote about mature women executives who in recessionary times had turned out to be the last consumer standing, taking on responsibility for both the financial and emotional well-being of multiple generations. The women in my cohort were defying the stereotypes of aging. We were acting, buying, and influencing just like younger consumers. No, scratch that. We were acting, buying, and influencing even bigger, better, and more than younger consumers.

Then I crossed the threshold of my sixtieth year and kept going. Somehow, I had not only arrived at "Can you believe I'm 62?" but was catapulting headlong towards "You look great for 63." Shockingly, my next birthday was going to transpire on the East Coast, thousands of miles from home, because my husband, Dan, had landed a job in NYC he couldn't refuse. Meanwhile, the start-up for which I was working virtually didn't care whether I was in California or New York. Before we could second-guess our decision, we put our beloved canyon cottage up for rent and moved east.

2

THE ELF

"EVERYBODY SHOULD LIVE IN NEW YORK AT least once in their lives," I told Maggie, my friend, an artist and the manager of a boutique that catered to the mature L.A. canyon crowd. Maggie and I had met a couple of years previously, having arrived at the entrance to the boutique at exactly the same moment; I needed a new jacket for my next book tour and Maggie was responding to the help wanted sign in the window. Her plan was to not only ask the owner for the job, but to hang her paintings for sale.

I had helped Maggie maneuver her unwieldy painting through the door, and by the time we reached the counter, our friendship had begun. I'd gotten the perfect jacket, and Maggie had gotten both the job and the gallery space. Each of us saw this as a good omen and decided to celebrate our successes together at Starbucks.

Two years later, I was back at the boutique, this time to say good-bye. Maggie took it surprisingly well. In fact, she saw my departure as a sign from God that she, too, was due for a big change. "We've got to make our sixties mean something," she'd said, rearranging her bangs in the three-way mirror, hiding a fast-growing crop of gray roots. Looking at our reflections, I caught a glimpse of her most famous painting, hung just behind us. It was the one of a garden elf that had been made into posters and that had graced most of the boutique customers' homes in the eighties, when we were busy decorating our first living rooms. The elf, an icon of eternal youth, had made her fame— but not her fortune. The latter had gone to an unscrupulous business partner, and, too, by the nineties, pictures of elves had gone sadly out of style. We had commiserated over many a grande latte since we'd met, as, despite my superb jacket, this latest book tour had been a dud. Self-help books for Boomer women had gone the way of elves, sad to say, as the market had turned first to chick lit and then to mommy porn.

Rather than spending long hours at her easel in her home studio, as Maggie had for most of her life, "the elf artist" was now managing a boutique and complaining about plantar fasciitis. And while still thinking of myself primarily as an author in her prime, who lived in a charming cottage in a canyon in Los Angeles, the truth is that I was working for a marketing Web site, poised to trail after my husband to a high-rise in New York.

3

SELF-IMAGE

ASIDE FROM COMMISERATING ABOUT MY impending birthday with Maggie, who was herself turning 60, I instinctively kept it quiet. Fifties is one thing. Sixties is another. Nevertheless, between crisp white shirts with the collars turned up and designer tortoise-shell glasses, I did think I looked good for my age. Increasingly, however, my blogs were betraying me. This betrayal started while I had still been in Los Angeles, and moved with me to New York, as I found myself writing more and more about simplifying rather than consuming and railing against costly anti-aging moisturizers that promised to keep us "forever young."

Then, one sad day, just a few months after the move, I went to the company Web site for which I had been serving as spokes-blogger, only to be introduced to the new poster girl for the cause. She could barely have been brushing fifty, and could pass for about thirty-five. What's more, her tone was unreservedly perkier than mine. And how could it not have been? Upon inquiry, I was let in on the scoop. The new spokeswoman for the Web site was a fictional avatar: the purchased image of a Photoshopped model given voice by staff members closer to my son's age. She was to author articles and interact with visitors over the Web, jobs I had previously undertaken with pride. But unlike me, she would never challenge young brand managers by suggesting that they refrain from saying things like "I know what older women want because I, myself, have a mother in her fifties."

Shortly thereafter, I received notice that while I had earned the unending gratitude and respect of my beloved CEO, he could no longer offer me employment. I understood that I would still play some smaller role in the firm. But nevertheless, here it was, in undeniable black, white, and pink slip: formal notice. I would dearly have loved to spend the rest of my life wallowing in self-pity, but the dog needed to be taken for a walk in the park.

4

JUST LUCKY

LUCKY ISN'T JUST ANY DOG. LUCKY IS OUR eight-pound Maltese-terrier mix, a "Morky." Bearing the best of both breeds, she has the coloring and vitality of a Yorkie and the soft, long hair and loving nature of a Maltese. And this wasn't any park either. This was McCarren Park in Williamsburg, the hippest hood in Brooklyn, just one subway stop from Manhattan. Not as big as Central Park, but clearly cut from the same cloth. Hardy grass, sturdy trees, and a dog barking up each post of a wire mesh baseball diamond fence because of the squirrel running along the top to first base.

Lucky was our dog, and McCarren was our park. We had just moved from corporate housing near Dan's Union Square office to a Williamsburg penthouse in a brand-new, pet-friendly building. From the patio of our seventh floor apartment, we overlooked the Manhattan skyline from across the East River. But better yet, we could walk out the front door, cross the street, and be chasing squirrels in the tip of the doorman's hat.

Yes, this was the second time in a handful of years I'd been laid off a job by a boss who purported to adore me. But this time—for the first time—I did not take this as personal rejection. I had worked hard over the years to build a spiritual safety net sturdy enough to catch my emotions when I fell. Just look how much I'd grown since my last downsizing, to be able to shake off something as onerous as being laid off and rather, to see this as an opportunity? I knew who I was—my value and my worth—and it was high time I started living life on my own terms. And as Lucky and I went on our daily walk, inspiration struck. Of course! So this was what this was all about. God was calling me to go back to writing full-time. Suddenly everything made sense. I even had the topic for my next book! It was all so obvious. And thanks to the pink slip, I would have plenty of time to write it.

I could see myself back with Oprah and on the *Today* show, offering my wit and wisdom. Plus, T-shirts, mugs, and baseball caps promoting my brand. Maybe a movie. And in this state of ebullience, life had once again become meaningful.

5

_____

FAME

EXUBERANT, I HEADED BACK TO THE PENTHOUSE
to begin writing. It was a Monday morning in October. Soon
Dan would be heading out to his new job, the one that had
instigated our move to New York a few months prior. He
put down the morning newspaper to give Lucky a pat and me
a kiss.

"Something tremendous happened on our walk," I
blurted out.

"That good?!?"

"Yes. I've got the topic for my next book."

"Hurray!" Dan said. "What's it about?"

"Dogs. Dogs and the meaning of life!"

"Dogs—and meaning?"

"Isn't this a terrific idea?"

Dan carefully picked the newspaper back up and reluctantly
turned Section D in my direction. There, in his unmistakable
branded blend of serene wisdom and cool glasses was a giant
photo of Deepak Chopra, his son, and his dog. The headline: "A
Lesson from Dad and Dogs."

Not just any dog, by the way. This, just like Lucky, was a
Maltese terrier mix. And this was not just any park. This was

Central Park, upon which McCarren Park had been modeled. And this was not going to be my book about dogs and the meaning of life. This was Chopra's dog, Chopra's park, and Chopra's book.

6

DEEPAK WROTE MY BOOK

EVEN AS THE FLICKERING FLAME OF HOPE struggled for one last gasp of oxygen, it was over.

Not just the publishing game. Any of the games I'd been playing all my life: the ascending spiral of success that I was absolutely sure had been building to the climax I'd not only deserved, but earned. Surely, the Chopras' book was more than an unlucky fluke. It was a betrayal. I will not put a brave face on this revelation. It was brutal, unfair, and a downright mean-spirited gesture on God's part.

However, after the moment of distress subsided, there came a most unexpected rush of emotion. Relief. For I suddenly realized that if Deepak wrote my book, I didn't have to write his, either. I was free not to write with hopes of becoming famous, or even getting published. I neither had to reap my harvest nor redeem my past.

I was also free not to have to hear my agent turn this book down because people aren't buying books by women over sixty who aren't celebrities, or worse—that my writing wasn't what it used to be. I didn't even have to come off as wise, clever, serene, or profound. In other words, I was free to do or write anything I wanted without worrying about whether it would mean anything to anybody else, live up to expectations, or make the publisher a single dime.

After twenty books, the truth has gradually been dawning on me that, despite the success as a writer I'd garnered over the course of my productive career, seeking fame was always at best a stand-in for what I have always really wanted: to trust that I already am and have enough, knowing that I'm connected to a meaning and purpose greater than myself without having to do anything particular about it.

At my age and stage in life, I no longer want to go the long way around for a crack at the real thing. I want to make every choice count because despite what anybody else thinks of me, no matter how marginalized or redundant in the world's eyes, I am here, I matter, and God loves me. There. I've spit it out, and I hope that by the end of this diary, I will be so centered in the truth of this, that I won't be shaken by, say, what happened this morning.

7

TEN LEGS

THE TRUTH IS I AM NOT FREE YET. FAR FROM IT. HOW do I know? Because even Lucky is better at calling the shots in her life than I am in mine. This morning, we went for a walk in the park and for a blessed half-hour, we thought only about the twitch of the squirrel's tail as we crept silently toward it. Lucky and I were a unit: six legs of stealth and elegance frozen in time. And then the bushy gray tail quivered and Lucky made her move. Held together by a leash, but so in tune there was not a hint of tension, we bounced together after the gray blur of fur. Just as we were about to close in on the squirrel, he disappeared up the tree. By the time we got there, the only sign of what had transpired was the shaking of leaves higher and higher in the branches.

This was one of those blessed moments of grace when heaven bends down to touch the earth and all is well. Lucky looked up at me, exultant at the chase and ready for more, but, having heard a ping on my BlackBerry, the moment passed. I had already disappeared into my e-mail, scanning my inbox for messages. While Lucky stood stock still with one paw in hunter's pose, waiting patiently on both the squirrel and me, I was swept away in an unpleasant exchange with someone whose opinion should no longer matter. There was also an e-mail from a prestigious magazine, but it wasn't a request for an interview. It was an offer to sell me an online subscription at a discount. And then, by God's grace, somewhere in my unconscious, a tail twitched, and I remembered myself.

Deepak can have that other book—the one I was going to write. This really is my crack at freedom.

8

CLOSE ENCOUNTERS

LUCKY IS STARING AT ME AS I WRITE, NOT AT all pleased. We have just come back from our second squirrel hunting adventure of the day, and while she has never yet caught a squirrel, she lives for the chase.

Even though she's mortified, having been forced to don a bright red boiled-wool coat with a black fake fur collar due to the first warning blast of wintery wind, she's a formidable huntress. I know she's spotted a squirrel when, after pulling me sled-dog style as fast as I can go, the leash suddenly goes limp. Lucky has frozen in place, nose pointed, paw up, willing to wait patiently as long as it takes for the squirrel she has spotted to make one wrong move. As soon as the squirrel spots Lucky, the two lock eyes. This can last anywhere from five seconds to eight minutes before the spell is broken by the squirrel's sudden lurch up a tree, through the slats of a fence or under a car, followed by a mad dash. Actually, it is possible that this could take much longer, depending on the squirrel's and my patience. But I promise you that it will never be Lucky who breaks her concentration first.

The main thing here is not the patience, which is admirable, but rather, the dog's instantaneously renewed enthusiasm. She does not mull, mourn, second-guess, ponder, or regret. And the only reason she looks doleful right now as I write is because, regardless of how many squirrels get away, she wants another chance.

This, of course, is also the only possible explanation for my own twenty books. I wanted to change the world. I wanted to call the shots in my life. And I wanted to be free. And while there have been blessed moments of feeling that my life's work has amounted to something—enough so that I had always felt it sufficiently worthwhile to give it another go—I recognize that I am in danger of giving up.

9

THE BARGAIN

THERE HAS NEVER BEEN A SQUIRREL ON OUR seventh floor deck, but Lucky is a true believer. Every time anybody cracks the door to the deck open, she makes a break for it. Reaching the rail, she dances up on her hind legs, certain that if only she can stretch high enough she will catch sight of a twitching nose or swishing tail.

Normally, Dan and I think this is funny. But not on this particular day. Dan was at work and I was glued to the weather channel, increasingly agitated by the beeps and flashing lights warning of a tornado that had been spotted north of Brooklyn, closing in fast. This being my first big storm in our exposed penthouse—one wall made mostly of glass—I grabbed Lucky up and hunkered down in the bedroom, with its small, secure window. Through slats in the blinds, I watched warily as the sky went from an eerie caramel to ash gray. Suddenly, there was a flash of lightning followed by the muted crash of thunder in the distance. I put Lucky under the covers—a barely discernible lump under the comforter.

The howling wind outside picked up speed, and through the slats I could see debris swirling up and over the railing like a dozen mini-tornados, backlit by the darkening sky. Then the lights went out, the room flashing on and off with each bolt of lightning, thunder roiling in one continuous roar.

"The cushions!" I shouted. Broken loose of their tethers, the outdoor covers had risen like mad ghosts off the patio furniture, billowing up and over the railing, and exposed cushions were flying everywhere. Rushing from the bedroom, I pushed the door against the resistant wind, just as the sky let loose a barrage of hailstones. I could barely keep my feet anchored to the deck as the icy stones stung my face. In a frenzy of pitch black rain, blinding light, and thunderous crashing, I grabbed the cushions that had not yet blown off the deck, the watering can, and a plant and hurried back inside. Then, soaking wet and shaking, I ran back to the bedroom to take refuge with Lucky. But in a flash of lightning, the awful truth dawned on me: there was no longer a lump in the comforter. When I'd cracked open the door to save the cushions, Lucky must have rushed outside.

"God no!" I shouted, running as fast as I could go. "Just let her be okay, God, and I'll do anything you ask of me. Anything." The response came swift and sure, as I caught glimpse of Lucky, the entire length of her body pressed against the glass door, her little legs up to her knees in pellets of ice. Through sheer force of will, I pushed the door open and pulled her back to safety, wrapping her shivering body in my arms. Lucky licked my cheek, her love and faith instantly renewed. I carried her to the darkest corner of the bedroom closet, wrapping her in a towel that had missed the clothes bin and landed on top of an unopened box.

Recalling the word I'd scrawled on the front of the box just before our move to New York, I instinctively understood the nature of the bargain I'd made with God, and exactly what it was I was being asked to do.

10

PRAYER SHAWL

AFTER DAN MADE IT SAFELY HOME THAT NIGHT and back to work the next morning, I retrieved the large unopened box I'd discovered in Lucky's and my place of refuge. This box, the one labeled "Spiritual," was the only box from the move to New York that had yet to be opened.

If ever there were a moment to pull it out, this was it. Throwing aside the hail-dampened towel, I dragged the box over the slippers and boots, and hoisted it onto the bed.

The contents welcomed me like an old friend. There was a little wooden foot rest I had purchased at a thrift shop years ago, converted into an altar. I lifted it out carefully and placed it in a corner of the bedroom. There were my copies of the I Ching, the Hebrew Scriptures, a book by Thomas Merton, and a few hand-typed, tattered pages of poems by the thirteenth-century mystic Rumi. I set them on top. There was a particularly meaningful rock I'd picked up during a two-week retreat in the desert and a perfectly shaped pinecone that for no rational reason had once moved me to weep with joy. I reached in and grabbed out my blue and white prayer shawl, placing it reverently around my shoulders. I lit the candle and the incense and retrieved the brand-new blank notebook

I'd purchased just before the moving van arrived, having had just enough time to scrawl in bold letters across the front: "Carol's Prayers." Finally, I put a favorite instrumental CD on the player and settled in to pray.

I sat quietly for one entire song. Waiting. Then an entire album. Nothing. Then I decided to watch some TV.

This is the real tragedy of age, as I see it. Ambition and faith that have held their breath for decade after decade, finally wheezing out as a long, resigned sigh.

WINTER

An aged man is but a paltry thing,
A tattered coat upon a stick, unless
Soul clap its hands and sing.

—WILLIAM BUTLER YEATS

11

LEFT BEHIND

THIS IS MY NEW ROUTINE: LUCKY AND I WALK DAN to the subway he takes to work in Manhattan. We watch as he descends the stairwell, Lucky refusing to budge until the last glimpse of him has definitively disappeared into the dark tunnel. Reluctantly, she turns her attention back to the street, slowly at first but quickly picking up speed because she has seamlessly traded in her experience of loss for a search for the perfect garbage can. As soon as she's selected her spot, she remembers the park and its squirrels, tugging at the leash as fast as we can go. For fifteen minutes or so, I forget that I am the only person in Williamsburg over twenty who has no other place I have to go.

As soon as we're back home, I sit down again at my altar to meditate. This lasts anywhere from fifteen seconds to two minutes before I grab Lucky and head down to the lobby for a complimentary Starbucks. If we're in luck, we'll bump into one of our neighbors and arrange a playdate for our dogs later in the day. More often than not, our young friends will be just heading out to work or play rehearsal or the recording studio, seizing upon the moment to ask if we'd occasionally check in on the dachshund Maxie or the terrier mutt Buster or the gentle pit bull with the improbable name of Daisy that lives just down the hall from us. The concierge, eavesdropping on the exchange, automatically punches my name into the approved entry slot, alongside a variety of housekeepers, cable repair personnel, and the occasional keg delivery man readying one apartment or another for a party. The dogs are invariably overjoyed to see any combination of us when the concierge buzzes us in.

That's pretty much it. Since Deepak wrote my book, I haven't had any new book ideas. Meanwhile, I am CEO of my own home-based company—but only halfheartedly so, as, while I will answer phone calls, I can't find it in me to initiate them anymore. I have no employees and since the phone hasn't rung recently, precious little work.

But this morning was not routine. I had heard on the news that there had been an ice storm overnight, and when I tried to go out on the patio to see for myself, the door was frozen shut. Peering through the crystals that turned our windows into a kaleidoscope, I could see the reflection of the cold sun off the deck, which had been transformed into a scaled version of the skating ponds I loved in my youth. It looked slippery and dangerous out there. But it never occurred to me to stay behind when Dan left for work. Dutifully, I put snow boots on Lucky's feet, then, taking turns: sweaters, hoods, and down jackets. We were ready. We loaded ourselves into the elevator, trailing behind Dan as he rushed through the front door heading towards the subway to work.

The moment my boot hit the icy pavement, I slipped. Not an all-out fall. But still, more than a mere skid. I stood there, checking to see if I was all there. A couple of twenty-somethings glided by in their Hunter boots as Dan reached back protectively to take hold of my arm. It was humbling. And suddenly, it seemed very stupid to risk a real tumble for, well, for nothing.

Even Lucky looked at me pitifully as we crawled back inside. Lucky is not used to me giving up like that. Nor to Dan leaving us behind. And in this moment, I realized what was really bugging me. It wasn't that at the very moment my career was supposed to have been peaking, I had been cast out of the mainstream's bosom nor that I was once again in an unexpected career transition. I already knew what that was all about, having gone through this several times before. Through sheer grit and determination, I'd always gotten things to work out sooner or later. But here's the rub. I suddenly found that I couldn't, in fact, muster my inner resources to do it all one more time. And, too, where was God now that I really needed help the most?

With a brutal mix of empathy and apology, Dan left me behind on the sidewalk as he forged steadily on to the subway. Standing there, I understood why I was feeling so lost. For this time, I wasn't just in the void, transiting to a new book topic or job. This time, I was transiting out of the peak of midlife and into old age. And at this new, unwelcomed stage of my life, I cannot risk a fall.

THE PARTY NEXT DOOR

AS IF I NEEDED ANY MORE CONFIRMATION THAT I had become suddenly old, I didn't have to wait long. Dan was working late into the evening when there came a knock at the door. The sharp rap was met by an explosion of barking as Lucky roused herself from my lap to protect us from intrusion.

"Is the party here?" Standing in my doorway was a young woman, perhaps twenty-five, with an artfully torn tank top and, tattooed on her shoulder, a skull and bones. Only then did I notice that down the hall, Claire—Daisy the pit bull's mom—had her door wide open. There was the sound of a raucous gathering in full swing. Daisy made a run for it, knowing that I'm always good for a treat.

Claire emerged to grab Daisy by the pink spiked collar and to beckon skull and bones to the appropriate portal. I was about to wave hello expectantly when I saw something I had never noticed before in my neighbor's young eyes. I had fed Daisy when Claire had been away, and she had taken Lucky squirrel chasing. Whenever we bumped into each other, we talked about our work, our favorite restaurants, and all of the other things that friendly neighbors do. And as we stood there, other neighbors continued to arrive on our floor, waving to me cheerily as they passed by to enter Claire's chamber. I saw all this. We witnessed all this together. And what I saw in her eyes that I'd never seen before was that she was embarrassed that she had not invited me to her party, and we both knew why. I am old.

Suddenly, this grown-up woman who imagines that she can gracefully accept the ups and downs, just happy to be alive, was knocked back into the self-knowledge that she could not even gracefully accept that she had not been invited to the party next door.

13

BEST FRIEND

IT'S TIMES LIKE THIS THAT ONE WISHES SHE HAD a best friend close by. Someone with whom she could grab a cup of coffee at the drop of a hat, parse the day's triumphs and tragedies, and help make sense of things. It seems like it's been years—but in truth, it's been only a matter of months—since the move from Los Angeles, remembering all those precious times I used to drop in on my friend Maggie that way. I knew that she was available at the boutique anytime between ten and seven. We socialized on occasion, too, Maggie and her husband, Greg, Dan, and I, getting together in Beverly Hills for steamed clams and in Santa Monica for walnut pasta. Greg was one of a handful of my friends' husbands that Dan liked: a professional peer and an affable conversationalist. Once, when he'd drunk one glass of Pinot too many, he bragged about having been a roadie for rock and rollers and their starlet girlfriends a couple of canyons over in his youth. But aside from the picture of a long-haired teenager on an ancient driver's license he carried in his wallet, there was absolutely no evidence that Greg had ever done anything more exciting in life than swim laps at the YMCA.

Our subject matter was always the same: where would

be better, cheaper, more fun, more satisfying to live at our age than L.A.? Maggie was drawn towards someplace warm and exotic, Thailand, maybe, or South America. Greg leaned more in the direction of a rushing river, anywhere in the world, where he could fly-fish. Our sacred text was the latest episode of House Hunters International, comparing the cost of purchasing a farm in Denmark with that of purchasing a converted barn in Bulgaria. We could all imagine a simpler life, with less clutter and busyness and more time for meaningful things. But until our sudden move to New York, it had all been just talk. Maggie and Greg were left behind on a whole other coast, and we'd moved in exactly the opposite direction from what we'd intended: straight into the heart of one of the most intense cities on the planet. To top it off, I have to admit that I'm not the best long-distance friend.

14

FACEBOOK

IT'S NOT THAT I DON'T CHERISH MY FRIENDS. I would love to have a good friend like Maggie in New York. Especially today, with the ice thickening and the possibility of my crossing the front stoop into the larger world feeling more and more unlikely. But having worked a series of big jobs in multiple locations over the decades, I have somehow evolved the definition of "good friend" to mean "someone who understands when you have to cancel lunch at the last minute because a client is in town." Maggie and I were like that. We understood when the boutique suddenly got a new shipment of belts in, or my boss had scheduled a last-minute conference call.

That is, of course, because the bulk of my career transpired before the advent of Facebook. Now, younger folks can keep their elementary school and summer camp friends for life, just by "Liking" their favorite songs and commenting on their new hairstyles. And, truth be told, I am kind of getting the hang of it myself. In fact, because of Facebook, I know that my daughter just bought herself a faux fur boa for her birthday in London, where she is pursuing her master's in arts management. I have tracked my grandson's progress in Tennessee from eating crayons to drawing with them. I have lightly followed the whereabouts of about 200 "friends" in the various cities Dan and I have lived in as we built our careers: Portland, Maine; Chicago, San Francisco, Napa, Nashville, and Washington, D.C., including an assortment of associates, networking buddies, fellow doctoral students, and extended family.

Housebound and feeling invisible, I chose to lay claim to the last of my bragging rights, taking and uploading a shot of the heavily frosted Manhattan skyline from our deck. Pleased with my post, I sat back to watch the response.

15

MESSAGE FROM CANCUN

IF I'D HOPED FACEBOOK WOULD CHEER ME UP, I was sadly mistaken. A recipe for golden beets posted by a young cousin at the same moment I'd uploaded my photo of the Manhattan skyline was now up to thirty-four Likes while my offering had stalled at one, which came from Dan, and even that only after hearing me cry about the popularity of my cousin's post and how nobody cared about me anymore. But that was the least of it. For as I scanned the day's posts for updates from friends, a strangely familiar face caught my eye.

I clicked on the photo, enlarging it so that I could get a better look. A young man and woman, wearing oversized sombreros, holding aloft bottles of Mexican beer, their arms around each other. Could have been an ad for Cuervo . . . but it wasn't. It was, rather, Maggie: "Having a blast in Cancun with my new friend Webster."

It had only been a matter of months since I'd said good-bye to Maggie and Greg in Los Angeles. Consumed with the move, and dealing with all the changes, I confess I'd neglected the relationship. But this wasn't the first time I'd fallen off the map, and I knew that Maggie—however bad a friend I'd been—would be happy to hear from me. Breaking my vow never to post again, I clicked the comment box and entered one word: "Webster?" Maggie responded immediately, although we were in different time zones. "Let's take this to e-mail, K?"

In short order, Maggie's e-mail arrived under the subject line: "Miracles." I started reading: "Carol, I want to thank you so much for inspiring me. After you left, I went into the doldrums. You're right about sixty—it's a bear. But then it occurred to me: I don't have to take getting older lying down. I started yoga and Pilates, and went to this fabulous doctor in Beverly Hills who put me on a designer brew of hormones. He told me about this amazing plastic surgeon in Mexico. To make a long story short: I booked a flight the next day, got my eyelids lifted, and met Webster. We've been together ever since. It's been over a month now."

That explained the vaguely familiar woman who smiled at me from under the sombrero. It was Maggie looking and acting like a teenager. But who was Webster? And what about Greg?

"Greg got laid off, came home, and started watching old episodes of *The Twilight Zone*. He said he was too old to take any shit anymore and that nobody would hire him anyway. When I left for Mexico, he had just watched 27 episodes of *The Twilight Zone* back to back. I don't think he noticed when I left."

"And Webster?"

"Isn't he awesome? Oh, there he is now, outside on his Vespa. We're heading for Pilates. I'll fill you in when we talk. Do you Skype?" And she was gone.

16

MAGGIE'S YEARBOOK

WHEN DAN CAME HOME, HE FOUND ME FACE down on the sofa. The only movement in the room was Lucky and I breathing in tandem, her little body rising and falling with each of my sighs.

As soon as I caught sight of Dan, my labored exhales ripened into quiet sobs. "Maybe she's right," I choked out. "Why would anybody want to get old when they could be drinking beer in Cancun with Webster?"

"What are you talking about?" Dan asked. "Who's Webster?"

"Here!" I hurled myself from the sofa to the computer and opened Facebook.

"What's that?" said Dan, falling guilelessly into my trap. "Is that a picture from Maggie's high school yearbook?"

"No, don't you see? That's Maggie now. She's not slipping on the ice and crawling back home to protect her brittle old bones. She's taking designer hormones and getting her eyelids lifted, and apparently she left Greg for this guy with a motorcycle in Mexico named Webster."

Dan looked confused.

"You want me to get a motorcycle?"

17

MY SPECIAL DAY

"WHAT YOU NEED IS A SPECIAL DAY," DAN SAID A couple of days later, after the ice had melted sufficiently for me to contemplate leaving the house, and what was really bugging me had sunk in.

"You should call one of your New York City friends to have lunch—and here," he reached into his briefcase and pulled out a gift certificate. One of the women at work had told him about a spa near their office, one of the best in Manhattan. Thinking it would cheer me up, he'd purchased the half-day "Revitalizing Package" for me, including a facial, massage, and unlimited use of the pool, hot tub, and sauna. His gift was not only sweet, but effective. I did, after all, have friends in New York going back twenty years, and the time had come to do something about that.

Ever since publishing my first book, I'd been collecting editors like charms on a Sweet Sixteen bracelet. Over the decades, I'd kept lightly in touch, my visits to the city occasions for celebration. There were steamed dumplings at a famous Times Square spot with Beth, the editor of my most recent business genre books. My second editor, Shelly, took the train in from New Jersey, and we dined on gourmet soups in the basement of Grand Central Station. Once every couple of years, there was blackened sea bass at my self-help books editor's favorite restaurant, where the waiter always reserved her a quiet table and I got to hear Marlene's best stories about her growing stable of celebrity authors. I watched my friends rise through the ranks of their publishing houses and careers, as we toasted each other's hard-won successes. Those were years full of promise, and a heady mix of business and friendship. I never suspected that it would end.

18

WITNESS TO A LIFE

SHE'S ONLY A COUPLE OF YEARS OLDER THAN me, but Shelly explained to me over the phone that she didn't get into the city much anymore. Especially not since the publishing industry had gone to hell. The last time she'd travelled in, it was to Book Expo, where she'd wandered the endless aisles looking for a familiar face. She'd been hoping to sell her wares as a freelance editor, but all she got was aching arches, and a burning question. Where was everybody? Was she really the last one of her generation of book people still standing?

She had picked up some intel from the trades, however. She had read that my business books editor had gotten a promotion, but it was a mixed blessing, as, due to the recession, she'd been simultaneously stripped of staff and resources. "Don't take it personally if you don't hear back from her," she told me kindly in our brief phone conversation.

She wasn't entirely right. I did hear back from Beth, but only long enough to tell me that she was too busy to meet. Shelly did have one promising bit of news for me, however. It was about Marlene, my editor at the largest and most prestigious of my publishers, whose career I'd tracked from the simultaneous signing of her first bestseller to the founding of her own imprint for the house. Along with Beth and Shelly, Marlene had been one of my best friends during the course of my publishing career.

Marlene and I had done multiple books over the years, shared personal stories, commiserating over everything from health and parenting issues to career highs and lows. Marlene was, the most of anybody, a witness to the breadth and depth of my career. Books may go out of print, but Marlene remembered when the most important thing in the world to me was whether we put a seashell or a lightbulb on the book jacket, and that the *Today* show had invited me on not just once, but twice.

My self-help books with Marlene, well-reviewed and with respectable sales, had come in both of our middle periods. I had ultimately moved on to doing marketing books with Beth in order to pay the bills, and Marlene had ended up chasing celebrities who had found God in rehab. But because we shared a passion for spirituality, and genuinely liked each other, she'd always extended the star treatment to me. It was with Marlene, toasting the publication of my fifth book with an expensed bottle of champagne, that I'd felt: "So this is what success feels like."

Now, for months, I'd been sending e-mails and placing phone calls to her that had gone unanswered. I'd assumed that, having moved on to her own imprint, like Beth she'd been dismissing my communications with a brief flush of fond memory, before moving on to more pressing matters.

"Don't you know," Shelly said. "Marlene's been let go. It was all over the trade media." Must I confess the truth? I was relieved. Certainly, at least, she'd now have time for an old friend.

19

OLD FRIEND

ONCE I SCORED HER CURRENT E-MAIL, IT WASN'T long before Marlene and I were back at her favorite restaurant eating blackened sea bass. The restaurant was serving a three-course prix fixe—more than I usually consumed in one sitting, but I was pleased by Marlene's choice. The moment I spotted her in the crowd around the reception desk, a wave of relief poured over me. She looked the same. And by that, I mean that unlike Maggie, she was not afraid to show her age. In fact, dealing with whether, how, and when to do something about the graying of our hair and the deepening laugh lines on our faces had been one of the topics we'd chewed on endlessly over the years, starting with the first gray hair that had sprouted on each of our heads during pre-publication of our first book together.

It had been Marlene who helped me develop my philosophy about aging: to be so self-secure in my value and worth that I could make independent, daring decisions about how I chose to present myself to the world. There she'd been, a master of the publishing universe, letting her hair go prematurely gray, taking pride in her aging face and plumping figure. She thought it leant her an air of gravitas. And I must say the look suited her well. By the very dint of going natural, she was proclaiming to the publishing world that she had arrived. She was now so powerful, talented, and daunting that she could even afford to look her age.

Inspired by Marlene, I had also dared myself to go gray, only to discover that my hair had no intention of turning into any kind of statement. Instead, each limp strand had simply faded into a shadow of its former self, giving the impression less that I had chosen to go gray, than that I had gone bald. I had bolted back to Maggie's boutique, where I had been handed the name of her hairstylist, who immediately turned my hair back to a sumptuous brown. His parting gift to me when I told him about our move to New York was the serial numbers off the two shades he blended to give me my proprietary look. Now here I was back in Manhattan sitting across the table from Marlene over our first course, feeling surprisingly self-conscious about my dyed brown hair despite the fact that she seemed to sincerely admire the shade. But never mind the chitchat, Marlene had something much more pressing to discuss.

20

LAST COURSE

THE FIRST COURSE, GRAVLAX WITH FESTIVE adornments, was an understandable venting of anger over having been "reorganized" out of her job. Somehow, in the shuffle, editors in their thirties got corner offices and imprint chiefs in their sixties got a cardboard box and an escort down the service elevator. I thought my story about being replaced by an avatar matched—or potentially trumped—Marlene's calamitous turn of events. But given that I still had a consulting agreement with the firm, no matter how fragile, my situation carried even less weight in our first-course conversation than did the capers rolling off our tiny forks.

Surely, the second course would be mine. Who better to process the tragedy of my pre-empted dog and the meaning of life book with than Marlene? I remembered fondly a lunch at this same restaurant during one of our books together when I was stuck on chapter six. Marlene, a wise and good friend as well as a crackerjack editor, had assured me that it would come to me. "Let it go for the afternoon. Go to the Met and take in the paintings and sculptures. Stop trying so hard and give it to God: the answer will come to you, when you least expect it." She'd been right. And I guessed that, should I be able to get a word in edgewise to ask for her advice, she could be right about me again. But the second course was Marlene's, too. She was going to show those jerks at the publishing house how stupid they'd been letting her go. In fact, she was in conversation that very afternoon with some important investors who were going to put up the money for her to start her own independent imprint.

I perked up. Marlene was, after all, a fan of my subject matter. In fact, she had repeatedly defended me over the years against the numbers guys who had been pressuring her to spend less time with authors of spiritual self-help books like me, and more time chasing notorious convicts and movie stars.

Perhaps all of this had been a lengthy preamble to her asking if she could publish my next book, to which I would respond by spending the third course telling her the ironic story about how Deepak had written my book, and how I was feeling surprisingly so free as a result. While breaking the hard chocolate off our third-course strawberries' backs, we would commiserate about having put in dedicated decades and made big money for our corporate overlords, only to be unceremoniously tossed aside. I could even entertain the luxury of telling her I'd think about her kind offer, and that of course, I could promise that my next book would absolutely be hers.

By the time dessert had arrived, I had convinced myself that saying all this would actually carry some weight and that there would, indeed, be a next book. That our long history together had amounted to something. But as fate would have it, the third course was Marlene's, too. She was rattling off the names of the famous authors she'd worked with over the years who owed her. She was going to systematically wine and dine them in order of the biggest sales numbers on down.

Apparently I was not one of them, for by the time the waiter brought the check, it had become painfully clear that each of us thought the other was going to pick up the sizable lunch tab. After an awkward pause, we split the bill.

I only heard from Marlene once after that, to tell me that the publishing deal had fallen through and she was thinking it was time for a change. Did I know the serial number of the shade of my brown hair?

21

DIS-ROBED

DAN HAD WANTED ME TO HAVE A SPECIAL DAY, and I was doing my best to oblige. The lunch with Marlene had been a dud, but maybe the revitalizing half-day spa treatment would deliver on its promise. The right kind of spa sets a mood as nurturing as a meditation retreat. With the altar I'd set up in my bedroom gathering dust, I desperately needed something to kick-start my spiritual life. I yearned for a connection to spirit. Soothing music. Candles. Loving, non-judgmental hands rocking me like a baby. I grabbed a cab and walked through the ornate front door, a special delivery package in dire need of careful handling.

"Hello!" I whispered in my best spa voice, trying to catch the model/receptionist's attention, which persisted in its commitment to checking e-mail messages and texts. After too long, she looked up at me as if I were lost: "Can I help you?"

I showed her the certificate, she handed me a key, robe, towel, and flip-flops.

"Do you have a bathing suit?" I asked. "I forgot to bring one."

"We don't use suits here," she replied. "But if you're uncomfortable with the idea, I can give you a second towel."

I grabbed the second towel and crossed the threshold into

the heart of the spa. Blue steam wafted up from a giant whirl-pool. Sipping cucumber juice, casually dangling their slender limbs into the hot water, were a stunning thirty-something mother and her sixteen-year-old daughter, both stark naked. A couple of model-thin twenty-year-olds, also in the buff, chatted amiably on a settee nearby. A young attendant, bless-edly clothed, guided me to my locker and invited me to disrobe for my treatments.

I looked around the spa, at all the young, proud flesh. No wonder the receptionist had thought I'd gotten lost. Not that I couldn't be prompted to remember when I, too, had felt om-nipotent with the beauty of youth. I remember that there were years, decades even, when I could enter a room, point my fin-ger, and turn heads.

As I aged, heads turned less and less often, and I do remem-ber a moment somewhere in my forties when I realized that I could no longer count on effortless magic to make me visible. But even so, lights turned low in the privacy of my own home, I could still revel secretly in the sheer physicality of being alive.

But strip down in full sight of the chorus of sylvan nymphs, knowing that in doing so, I would be offending the integrity of the moment with an assortment of extraneous rolls of fat, out-of-control sags, a prominent scar across my chest, and various other incongruent reminders of mortality?

The girl sensed my hesitation. "Don't be nervous," she said kindly. "Nobody will notice you."

22

JOURNEY BY FLASHLIGHT

IT IS POSSIBLE THAT SOME OF THE PEOPLE ON LinkedIn think I've gone missing simply because I'm engaged in some big marketing project that required a non-disclosure agreement. But the truth is that by allowing myself to grow old and of little practical use to anyone, most of my peers are probably not thinking much about me at all. Twenty books, corporate titles like senior vice president, co-chair, and chief strategist, my impressive resume of media appearances, and even my doctorate—all swallowed in the void. There are little deaths every time I check my e-mail and it's only how much Angie's List misses me.

Somehow, I have managed to get up this morning, relying on sheer will and determination to at least go to the altar and pretend to pray. Instead, I found myself re-running the lunch with Marlene, the exchange with Maggie about Webster, and what I now think of as "the spa incident" over and over again in my mind. I am not sure whether to be proud or ashamed of myself for having tried so bravely to get on with my life. Frankly, I don't trust determination, grit, drive, discipline, or any other of the many skills I've perfected over the years, and that have brought me to this place. It was grit, after all, that I'd called upon to get through my visit to the spa.

Bypassing the pool, hot tub, and sauna, I had managed to sneak from my locker to the room for facials, only to be told that the treatment that was included in the "Revitalizing Package" was actually intended for younger skin. Pinching my neck and cheek, the facialist, an icy Russian, suggested that what I really needed was more along the lines of "Resurrection," an emergency anti-aging organic peel and a microdermabrasion treatment with two types of collagen firming masks, available for a couple of hundred dollars more—"but worth it." When I demurred, I was instead persuaded to upgrade to the "Rejuvenation Special," guaranteed to reverse years of aging at half the cost. Whatever soothing effects would have otherwise come about from the gentle exfoliation were offset by the sales pitch that had taken to relentlessly repeating itself in my mind throughout the entire treatment. "Look," she had said, holding a magnified mirror up to my face. "You really don't want to look this tired."

Between the slip on the ice, lunch with Marlene, and the spa incident, I am reminded how conflicted I am about pushing myself once again, even for an admirable purpose: the attempt to wrest meaning out of my life on the eve of turning yet another year older.

23

THE EXPLODING FISH

AND THEN, A FISH EXPLODED ON ME. A FISH conceivably could have exploded on me at any earlier age of my life, or on a younger individual. But in the escalating countdown to my birthday, I'm taking this particular fish personally. "You are incompetent," the reheated salmon bits screamed at me, shooting out of the microwave door like heat-seeking missiles. "And foolish."

All I did was open the door to the microwave as I have done a million other times before with no incident. But this microwave was not resting on the counter like my trusty oven back in Los Angeles. Rather, this one hung down from the cabinet next to the fridge at precisely face height. Just as I opened the door and peered in to check on the salmon's status, a fatty fin burst apart and covered me with burning bits of pink and silver.

Having entered the dark, endless tunnel into old age, this as well as every other incident, ailment, or flaw is experienced as an accusation. Stinging me to tears, each splatter point of scale, meat, and tail left a tiny, burning blister: one in the shadow of my nose, another on my chin, a spray of blister fin holes across my upper chest. It could have been worse. But still, I should have known better.

You don't go face-first to inspect a sizzling plate of salmon in a head-level microwave oven any more than, say, what my mother did late in her culinary history. She'd left a pot of soup on an open flame boiling so high, hard, and long on the stovetop that the liquid evaporated completely, and the vegetables turned black and then started to smoke, setting off the fire alarm. Dabbing at each of my stinging spots with butter on a knife, I painfully recalled getting the dreaded call from her apartment manager telling me that her forgetfulness was worrisome to them and that they respectfully suggested, then demanded, that she be relocated to a living situation in which she was less likely to burn the building down. Before we knew it, we were sitting in the midst of all the things that defined her life, packed away in boxes, waiting for Salvation Army before we walked out the door with two small suitcases, headed to assisted living.

There, I've said it. A fish explodes on a younger person. "Damn fish." "Damn oven." But this fish—this explosion. I walked to the bathroom, wiping frazzled fish guts off my clothes and skin, rubbed aloe vera on the reddened wounds, and cried to the reflection of my own mother in the mirror: "Damn it. You're losing it."

24

BOILED CHICKEN

ASIDE FROM FIN- AND BULLET-SHAPED REDDISH spots under my nose and sprayed across my chest, I am otherwise a healthy, vigorous woman experiencing what my doctor considers to be the normal wear and tear associated with aging. I once snuck a peek at his chart, and saw what he'd written down to describe my general demeanor. "Well-nourished."

Well-nourished from the outside, maybe. But inside, there is now a black hole that is filled to the brim with the latest age-related ailment to add to my growing litany of complaints. Somewhere between my stomach and my esophagus, a little flap I had always previously taken for granted has gone flabby. There was a time, not long ago, when I could drink my coffee black, eat my pizza slathered in tomato sauce and my chocolate cake gooey with fudge filling, and fall asleep redolent and peaceful. Today, a repast along these lines would send me to the emergency room. I'll take the occasional Tums, the Pepcid AC, but I have now replaced my compulsion to lose those last ten pounds with my compulsion to avoid adding any more medicine to my burgeoning regime of drugs: Boniva for osteopenia, Crestor for cholesterol, Ocuvite to stave off macular degeneration, and Osteo-Force, the mother of all calcium pills. There's also Advil for when my back goes out and Listerine mouthwash to keep the enamel on my teeth white and strong. So yes, add this to my list: I'm now eating like an old person: applesauce and skinless boiled chicken. But not tomorrow. Tomorrow is my birthday and I am determined to savor every single bite.

25

BOOTIES

I MUST LEAVEN THIS RECORD OF MY JOURNEY BY telling the truth that there are still those times when age is not an issue. Usually, my awareness of needing nothing, asking nothing is momentary. I will be measuring rice to put into boiling water, or putting snow booties on Lucky, when out of nowhere, the sensation that all is right with me and with the world sweeps through me like a flush of warmth, as spontaneous as a shiver, and as fleeting as well. Capturing such a moment, I have rushed to my diary to write today, swept forward on a wave of gratitude. Or, to be more precise, cresting aloft a white foam of relief. Not in celebration of my birthday—which was yesterday—but because thank God almighty, my birthday is finally over.

I'd intended to journal on the anniversary of my birth, and anticipated that I would be talking about the in-breaking of the divine. My birthdays have almost always carried with them a scent, a sense, a celebration of God's presence. Perhaps this was in part because of the way February 6 falls in the progression of seasons. Every year, growing up in a suburb of Chicago, I planned an ice skating party at the outdoor rink that magically appeared winter after winter in the playground behind my public school. I loved the freedom of putting blade to ice, skidding, swirling, and sliding round and round with my friends. I loved to huddle in the little club house over a jug of hot chocolate, prepared and poured by my mother. Nothing can match the anticipation of opening gifts in the chilled air. And even though there were no bonfires allowed, I could smell the tangy smoke heaving out of chimneys from neighborhood homes. I lived for my birthday.

And every year, beginning January 1, I'd start praying for the ice to last because inevitably, the day before or the hour before my birthday, the snowflakes would suddenly give way to raindrops, and the slick, solid ice upon which we'd depended all winter, would start to get mushy around the edges. Sometimes on February 6, a rope would be hung across the entrance and we would be told that the rink was closed. A line of cars would follow our Rambler wagon dutifully home, where we'd still sip hot chocolate from jugs poured by Mom. Instead of watching us fly across the ice, my dad would be showing us reel-to-reel Mickey Mouse cartoons in the basement.

Remembering this story this time around bears with it a particularly poignant sense of the bittersweet. I am reminded that expectation and disappointment are as much a part of the progression of the seasons of my life, as are visitations of the divine. And yesterday, rather than the flush of the sacred I assumed would be mine, I melted slowly but surely into a gentle melancholy.

26

SKYPE

AT THE TIME, I COULDN'T FIGURE OUT WHAT had been causing the dissonant birthday sadness. After all, I'd had a series of loving phone calls and e-mails from friends and family. Dan brought me flowers before I'd even gotten out of bed. In my honor, Lucky sported a pink bow in her hair and licked my nose. Maggie sent me an invitation to Skype. When we connected later in the day, I told her that I had hit a surprisingly rough patch and wondered if I'd done the right thing moving to New York. "Of course you did," she said. "It was such a brave thing to do. You'll get the hang of it, you always do. Meanwhile, I'm proud of you, girlfriend! Happy Birthday!"

When I asked how she was doing, she grinned from ear to ear, explaining that the hormones had given her the libido of an eighteen-year-old. "You've really left Greg for Webster?" I inquired, hoping to keep any judgment out of my voice, but worried about her response. After all, Greg was a friend, too. The Skype visual stalled just as her grin froze into a grimace, the audio of her perky voice dissonantly soldiering on. Whispering now, she confessed that she was running out of the designer pills that were only available in the U.S., plus Greg was begging her to come home. Moreover, she'd been keeping the meds a secret from Webster, who, it turned out, was a New Zealand company's organic vitamin rep she'd bumped into at the clinic after her plastic surgery. Webster was adamantly opposed to people putting chemicals in their bodies but was someone who, in unwitting combination with the meds, made her feel sixteen again. Plus, she was thinking about painting again. After Skype crashed a couple of times, we caught one last electronic pulse just long enough to profess our undying friendship, saying good-bye and that we'd send each other loving thoughts.

Late afternoon, the neighbor children stopped me in the lobby to sing "Happy Birthday to You" in their native languages, French and Egyptian. Dan took me for dinner with friends. Atop my favorite birthday cake was a single candle, too dim to ward off the bittersweet aura of the day.

27

THE END OF THE STORY

THE RELIEF THAT ACCOMPANIED THE BLESSED cessation of happy birthday greetings was short-lived as I began getting a grip on what had really been bothering me. In brief, I'd become tired of my own story. No: more than that. I was not just tired of my story, but of narrative in general.

How many times in one's long life can the heroine of the story be faced with challenges that upset the status quo? She draws upon internal and external resources to process the events, questions previous assumptions, and breaks through to new levels of understanding. The drama pivots on crisis and resolution, the lead character emerging in the end with enhanced power and potential. I feel good about myself, others are inspired, and one day an e-mail arrives from a total stranger, telling me any one of my twenty books—lent to her by a friend, borrowed from the library, or purchased secondhand—has saved her from despair. I have previously been so convinced that this is the aspirational arc of the well-lived life that on the final page of my last memoir, I concluded that "God must love a really good story."

Over the course of my birthday, I'd forged ahead with my story arc out of habit, as if detailing my efforts to come to terms with my lack of ambition, my ruminations about age and stage with friends and family contained some pithy seed of implied meaning. Some heard about how slippery it is outside. Others heard about the exploding fish. But the truth was that there had been growing anxiety every time the phone rang. For it had become increasingly challenging to sound like my old self. Irony and paradox had worn thin as I made increasingly feeble attempts to turn pathos into revelation. Surely, even this mood could be placed in the context of the arc of narrative. But mid-story, I found that I could not muster anywhere near enough dramatic tension to redeem what turned out to be my birthday dialogue. Stripped of my struggles with work, ambition, or writing my next book; having reluctantly moved beyond needing to guide my children into the right schools and careers; having long ago left behind the excitement of falling in love, getting married, building a life together, and now bereft even of God's reassuring presence. I'm old, okay? What else did anyone need to know?

28

ORDINARY HAPPINESS

THREE DAYS INTO WRESTLING WITH MY birthday slump in the pages of my diary, I put my pen down, vowing never to write again. Of course, the notebook "Carol's Prayers" was still blank. Lucky and I had already gone squirrel hunting and down to the lobby for coffee an embarrassing number of times. Blessedly, on the last trip down, the doorman had handed me a package from FedEx. It was a birthday gift I'd ordered for myself a week ago; its arrival couldn't have been more timely.

I could no longer write. That was true. But I could still read. I unpacked the book and admired the cover. The book was titled *Magic of the Ordinary* by Gershon Winkler. Based on the reviews I'd read, Gershon was the grown-up Jewish equivalent of a modern-day Huck Finn, wanting nothing more than to float down the river on his handmade raft, damn the consequences.

What had attracted me to the book were the reviews, admittedly not pretty, but enticing, nevertheless. Apparently, Gershon had ticked off a lot of people when, facing a life stage crisis, he walked away from the entanglements of both his family and his leadership role as a rabbi in the Orthodox

Jewish community in Brooklyn. But in my current mood, his rebelliousness of spirit was a big part of the appeal. For here is a man who does not spend much if any time regretting the past. Gershon moved from his prestigious position in Brooklyn to a cabin in the rural wilderness. Sustaining himself through odd jobs and living off the land, Gershon initiated a new life off the grid. In place of electricity and running water, he set out to acquaint himself with "the magic of simply being."

"The clues concealed in Creation are not about what you need to be doing or where you need to be going, or what choices you need to be making," writes Gershon. "Those sorts of questions belong more to what tangle us than to what frees us. These sorts of questions are irrelevant . . . because they distract us from the gift of the moment." Gershon admits that not only did he not resolve his life stage crisis, he didn't even try. "The confusion in my head was nowhere to be found. I was finding no answers because I had lost all the questions."

Like Gershon, I long to stand at the center of my universe, embodying the mysteries that defy the status quo. I want freedom that is a merger, an integration—a transcendence and a sinking into. And most of all, I would like to look forward to the possibility of living forever in that moment of peace that descends when you have read the last words and gently closed the cover of a great book.

But who am I fooling? I can appreciate, admire, and crave that place of freedom that Gershon has paid so dearly for. But after all the pages had been turned, when I put his book down, I was confronted with one more question. Am I so deeply embedded in the old paradigms that I will never escape into the profound freedom of intimacy with God I crave?

I am determined to at long last give my life permission to

be whatever it chooses to be. My life may be very quiet and un-eventful. My life may at times rise to new heights of emotion. Whatever my post-story life turns out to be, I will not aim to inspire, entertain, or educate, and neither will I be concerned about disappointing or pleasing.

But do I truly have the courage to let my life find its own ca-dence, weaning myself from the compulsion to live large? What would a life without complaining, yearning, crisis, and break-through actually be like?

29

EVOLUTION

SIXTEEN DAYS SINCE I LAST WROTE. PERHAPS the mystic in me was afraid to take note of the possibility of letting life find its own rhythm, lest it roll off the knife's edge like capers down the drain. But, to tell the truth, I was also smarting from having offered advice to one of my adult children, which I know better than to do. Eventually we reconciled—we always do. But I sorely miss the intimacy of parenting young children, sitting in the stands at plays and at soccer games, helping with homework, teaching to drive and then maintaining control over the keys. This was the sweet elixir of power and the busy illusion that what I said, did, and hoped for them could somehow save them from living a real life.

The missing sixteen days were not so much an absence as a lull, a presence so subtle that it did not register. Not that I wasn't busy. Carrying a handful of entrusted keys, Lucky leading the way, I once again called on neighbor dogs whose young masters left them alone all day to go to work. For a couple of those days, Claire had gone on a business trip and we'd taken Daisy in, making sure both the dogs got plenty of walks and healthy treats. I checked my e-mails, gathered receipts for our budget envelope, and reluctantly agreed to an interview with *Ad Age* about marketing to Boomer women. I also wrote the handful of blogs for which I was still being paid, stubbornly dodging expectations that I tell the story that marketers want to hear. I find myself unwilling to compromise, and fatalistic about the possibility of losing even the spare change that is being thrown my way.

The argument with my offspring was hard to shake off. We made up, but not before I was forced to confess—not for the first time—that while I had always thought that I was a stellar parent, mistakes had been made. By now, the litany of complaints is mostly familiar to me, and I comfort myself by remembering that I have accomplished something in the course of my life—call it evolution—that my brittle mother never did: apologizing. Of course, I am only too willing to apologize for more than I know I probably should. The chief complaint against me, by the way, is that I apologize too much, for which I'm extremely sorry.

30

BUDGETING

LIFE ON THIS SIDE OF SIXTY CONTINUES IN A mostly undifferentiated flow, as if much of the drama of my life has faded to vague: time not unpleasant but with precious few contours. I'd think this is what peace feels like, but for the fact that the altar continues to stand in mute testimony to my inability to pray. The sun sets. Then I get Dan's call telling me he's leaving work and it's time for Lucky and me to walk to the subway on Bedford to fetch him. And in the many hours between? Life unobserved but flowing. Where exactly did the time go?

There are twinges, of course. For after a life of big achievement, what do I actually have to show for myself? I have been interviewed by so many publications so many times, the interview with *Ad Age* is incorporated into the flow of the day with only the slightest ripple of pride or pleasure. Instead of ambition, there is a Greek chorus muttering: "Never again," and "Screw it." No e-mails or texts from the kids, either. Rather, what little satisfaction emerges from the fog comes to me from a most unexpected source. I have become obsessed with keeping our budget. Of course, the degree of persistence with which I teach myself to manipulate numbers is directly proportional to the amount of income I have stopped contributing to our retirement fund.

Only now, after six decades on overdrive, do I realize that there is and has always been an alternate route to the fear-driven ambition that has marked the many decades of my life. Add up what is coming in. Spend less than that.

31

UNHINGED

AFTER GERSHON'S BOOK, I HAVE GONE ON A reading binge. Not religion or philosophy, but *The Idiot's Guide to Budgeting* and *Investing for Dummies.* The altar in the corner is now stacked with yellow pads and calculators. When I'm not reading, I scan the Internet for free budget programs, entering best guesses onto sample graphs for how much we spend going to movies and buying treats for Lucky. I am learning as I go, pushing the programs for more data sheets to populate. Determined, I sign up for a free trial of a budget program featuring an Excel-powered chart that holds the promise of mastery. I feel proud, daring, brave when I convert the trial membership into an actual purchase. I now belong to something larger than myself.

Numbers take over my computer screen, and with a level of ambivalence and lust normally associated with pornography, I issue forth at last the word that dare never be spoken aloud: *retirement.*

I am part of a generation, after all, who has always said that we will never retire. We are too vital, too youthful, too engaged. We turn our noses up at our parents' version of retirement, a self-chosen retreat to golf courses and rocking chairs. Our generation will not be herded to the margins, no matter how well-manicured, even if we could afford to go, which is increasingly unlikely.

If you were to ask me if I want to retire, I'd say "no." I wouldn't even think about it or hesitate. "No. I don't even like to play bridge. (Or go fishing or rock on the front porch.) No, I'm not willing to voluntarily surrender my hard-won power."

But ask me if I'd like to be free to make my own choices about if and who I work for, when, and why—and there's no question. Give me a cabin off the grid, one without electricity and running water if that's what it takes. Also a porch and yes, a chair that rocks, slides, and swings if I so choose. I may not be ready to admit that I want to retire. But I do want to be free.

32

AT THE BORDERLINE

IT HAS BEEN SHEER GRACE TO HAVE BEEN able to throw myself into something concrete and tangible, something with a beginning and an end, like the numbers that my life generates on a daily basis.

At this point, with Dan working at the peak of his career, our numbers are black and bold. But if Dan were to answer the urge towards freedom, then what? Surely if not now, someday we will both want to choose how we spend our days. So day after day, I continue to busy myself working through receipts, invoices, and e-bills, entering the figures into neat columns in the newly purchased budgeting software. There are side trips to online calculators and calls to the Social Security office, our new financial adviser, and our new CPA for clarification. I've been asked how long I'm going to live, and between Dan and me, who is going to go first. I do my best to come up with something midway between pathetic and greedy regarding how many years I say I think I've got left. And then peering deep within the gears of Excel, the numbers begin to coalesce into a picture of my life past, present, and future. Day after day until at last, there is one last receipt to enter and something that has been complicated, mysterious, and troubling is suddenly revealed with all the precision of the orbiting planets.

We are borderline. We may have enough to retire based on what we've saved, the entitlements we've earned, what Dan's making, and what we expect to spend in the future. In fact, we probably do. But it is not this information that threatens to end the hypnotic flow of these past weeks. Rather, it is that the quest to master budgeting, the all-consuming mission that has given my days meaning and purpose, is coming to an end.

33

WHACK-A-MOLE

EVEN AS I CELEBRATE MASTERY OVER OUR numbers, I find that I've been bracing myself for life to begin asserting itself again. Despite the fact that I have been journaling, reading, and thinking about the onset of aging nonstop, it feels as if I've forgotten something. No, not really something: everything. What will I do with my time this afternoon? What is it that will keep me both entertained and fulfilled today? And not just today, what about tomorrow, the day after, and ten or twenty more years from now?

It is ironic that one of the most anxiety-free times of my life was after the shock of being diagnosed with breast cancer fifteen years ago. After the denial, anger, and mourning, acceptance of my mortality settled loosely about me, like the hospital gowns I donned during my many visits to doctors. Butt to the wind and devil-may-care. I had been released from all my everyday concerns: no need to worry about whether I was contributing enough to assure our future. What future? Did we have enough money for retirement? Weak and baldheaded, would I even ever work again, let alone retire? How about entitlements like Medicare? Or was it suddenly a waste of time bothering to check actuarial tables, given the tight race between Joe Black and fiscal conservatives threatening to make the eligibility age for Social Security a moot point for me? In place of the constant calculations, there was a sudden, blessed emptiness. Towards the end of chemotherapy, I recall suddenly becoming feverish and weepy. Dan came to sit by my side, wiping my brow.

"What is it?" he asked, concerned.

"You know, Dan, I always hoped I would emerge from this experience with something tangible I could put my hands on. You know, I'd trust that this cancer would never come back or that I had somehow won. But it's not like that at all. I know now that I have no idea what the future might bring."

"No wonder you're crying! That sounds scary!"

"No, you don't understand! I'm crying because I don't want to forget this feeling of absolute freedom. I know it, deep in my bones, that God has been with me through everything and knowing this, I believe that anything's possible and everything's all right."

And then I got better. The tests came back normal. Eventually, life reasserted itself and my spiritual immersion was over. I knew I was healing when I started worrying about stupid stuff again, like whether I was using more cell phone minutes than I'd planned and if it was time to change the filters on the air conditioner. I was back in the world of logistics, deadlines, irritations, and anxieties, realizing that I had a choice. Did I want to re-enlist in life with all its demands, uncertainties, complexities, and ambiguities? Or did I want to float off down the river like a pretty little leaf? That was fifteen years ago.

I'm still here. I'm anxious. Tossing and turning in bed, I am restless with the possibility that I am still vital enough to catch the wind in my sails. And even if so far the only direction I've been taken in is to the tumble of blankets wrapping around my kicking legs, I've apparently decided that the price of living is worth it.

34

KEEN INSIGHTS

LAST MONTH I HAD GERSHON WINKLER AS MY guide. Now I have stumbled across the work of Sam Keen, whose *Hymns to an Unknown God* has been on my shelf for years. This book has somehow made it through multiple moves as Dan and I have followed various career opportunities, from its original home in California, to Nashville, to Maine, back to California a couple of times, Washington D.C., and now New York. In addition to the few sacred texts that made it into the box marked "spiritual," there is only one small box worth of books that has passed this most stringent of critiques, all others having succumbed to their fate in the dime pile at one of many garage sales over the years.

The book fell off the shelf as I reached for incense, an accident that feels to me to have been divinely ordained, as it turns out that when I purchased the newly published book fifteen years ago, Sam was about the same age as I am now. I do recall having liked the book a lot the first time through, viewing Sam as a sage and worldly elder. But this time, as I read the book grown-up to grown-up, I feel both chastened and inspired by his spiritual maturity. My eyes are drawn to multiple passages, underlined in my youth and ripened exquisitely by time.

"We assume that we are entitled to a life without loneliness, anxiety, fear, want, or abuse of any kind," Sam writes. Rather than blame others or attempt to escape or transcend, Sam suggests that the route to freedom comes from a far less entitled place.

"Each of us must make a fundamental philosophical decision about how we are going to understand the flawed, faulted, broken character of human existence . . . Is it due to hardness of heart, rebellions, and disobedience to the will of God?

"Have we betrayed ourselves? Is it neurosis, a split between grandiose and debased images of the self that causes us to neglect our real self? Is it a wound that is the result of childhood abuse and faulty parenting?

"Is it because I am an adult child of an adult child of an adult child of an alcoholic, wealthaholic, workaholic, religionaholic?

"Is it a chemical imbalance or a genetic abnormality? Is it alienation that comes from living in a capitalistic, consumeristic, competitive economy?

"Is it due to maya, illusion, ignorance of my true (non-egoic) nature? Is it an ontological wound that comes with human self-consciousness, imagination and inevitable self-judgment by standards we ourselves erect?"

Because I resonate with Sam and his fierce questioning, I grant myself the generosity to hope that I am also entering my years of spiritual maturity, bearing the fruits of a lifetime of seeking, sensing the faintest possibility of wisdom.

In any case, I believe I have the answer to Sam's questions.

The answer is "Yes."

35

MAGGIE'S VISIT

FIRST THERE WAS A FACEBOOK MESSAGE, THEN we took it to e-mail, then Skype—then on yet another of a long string of snowy days, there was the anticipated phone call from Maggie. She was at Penn Station and would be coming over to the apartment within the hour.

From the tone, content, and quantity of communications, I had a good idea of what to expect. And it wasn't good. In a nutshell, Maggie had gotten a frantic call from her only sibling, a younger brother in Philadelphia. Their ninety-year-old mother had fallen and broken her shoulder. She was on medication, and the pain was under control. "She's been asking for you," her brother had said. "And, I really could use your help."

By the time Maggie had flown from Mexico to Philly, her mom had also picked up a urinary tract infection requiring even more meds. She'd been moved from the hospital to a nursing home where Maggie had found her lying on a railed bed, slightly delirious. Nevertheless, the minute she'd walked in the room, her mother had lit up with recognition. Maggie was overwhelmed with relief to see that not only was her mother alive, but that she knew who Maggie was.

Any initial jubilation was worn away day by day as, for the entire duration of Maggie's several weeks' visit, her mom had been stuck ricocheting between two equally upsetting modes. In Mode Number One, she angrily blamed Maggie's brother for depriving her of the means of killing herself, begging Maggie to administer to her a lethal dose of drugs. In Mode Number Two, Maggie's mother sang "Oh My Darling Clementine" over and over again, a manic grin on her face. In Mode Two, Maggie's mom would occasionally grab her daughter's hand, look deeply into her eyes, and whisper: "Thank you for taking such good care of me. You were always the one I could count on," before bursting back into another round of Clementine.

In her own seesaw way, Maggie's mom had for the foreseeable future become stable. And, grateful for the several weeks of reprieve, her brother was ready to take back control of the situation. Maggie, free to leave, determined to stop by New York en route home for a much-needed debrief with a good friend.

36

DEBRIEF

HOURS AFTER LEAVING PHILADELPHIA, MAGGIE was on our sofa, pale, exhausted, and looking much older than the last time I'd seen her. Her skin had lost its luster, and her hair had turned completely gray, arranged into an unruly presentation of checkered headband, short spikes, and flyaway bits.

From the e-mails, texts, and Skype, I knew some of what was going on, as if her mother's critical condition weren't enough. As feared, for instance, she had run out of the designer hormones. She'd finally confessed to Webster the secret to her eternal youth. After threatening to leave her for her deception—"I had no idea you were sixty"—Webster gave into her pleas to stay. In fact, he had pulled together an alternate regimen consisting of Chinese herbs and infusions, flown in from New Zealand and provided to her at cost. Plus, he insisted that she stop dying her hair because of the chemicals. Then, too, there was Pilates, yoga, and t'ai chi. Despite their best efforts, Maggie had suffered a menopausal-style backlash culminating with the urge to jump off the balcony of a rooftop restaurant.

She hadn't, of course. But when the Chinese herbs failed, and by the time her gray roots had completely overtaken her hair, Webster had already moved on to somebody his own age. It was then she'd gotten her brother's call. After a couple of glasses of wine, seated on the sofa of my apartment in New York, only then did she admit that she'd greeted her brother's plea to come to Philadelphia with a guilty flush of relief.

"I was screwing up every which way. Webster dumped me, and what was I thinking, anyway? Greg knew something was up, I mean, how long does it take to recover from an eye lift normally? I just wish Greg would have gotten pissed at me—anything other than sit at home in front of the TV drinking beer. Before I left for Cancun, the worst thing in his world was when the cable went out. I wasn't even sure he'd notice if I'd gone missing. We hadn't had sex in months. And who can blame him. I'm a great big zero. A nothing who is going to end up with nothing."

37

WITHDRAWAL

BETWEEN WITHDRAWAL FROM THE HORMONES, complicated, of course, by Webster's rude departure and confrontation with her mother's upsetting condition, Maggie was a mess. "I'm being punished," she'd cried quietly through her tears, railing off a list of transgressions. She was guilty for leaving Greg, for not being there for her mother when she'd needed her, for her blown career as an artist, and for lying to Webster. But with all that, I still sensed that there was something more she wasn't saying. I took her hand, letting her know that I was still with her, just listening.

"I always try to do my best," Maggie continued. "But it's as if the universe were saying there's something wrong with my very essence. How else can you explain that I was given my career and then it was taken away from me? How could I be so deluded to think I'm worthwhile, that I have something, anything to contribute? What if the whole world is right about me?"

"Maggie, you're a wonderful painter. Just think about how many of your paintings are out there in the world, cheering people up."

"But people don't buy real art anymore. It takes me 100

hours to do an original painting, and people can't afford to pay for my time, even if they did like my subject matter, which they don't. They think gardens and elves are corny. Imagine elves being corny! They'd rather rip something edgy off from Google images and turn it into their new screensaver. Something with fangs and dripping blood. God, I feel so damned old."

"You're not the only one, Maggie. The same thing happened to my whole class of self-help authors. I never thought the brightest and best of our generation would go the way of the buggy whip. Everything's changed—eBooks, computer graphics, public domain photographs. It's happening so fast, even thirty-somethings feel old."

"I should have worked harder at keeping up, but after a day of work at the boutique, I'm exhausted. All those middle-aged women those ads show with their boundless energy. They're on ski lifts and running companies. Hillary Clinton racing around the world, for God's sake. There must be something missing in me, something fundamentally wrong. I'm never going to beat this. I just don't have what it takes."

Suddenly, I realized that we were talking about more than Google images and digital design. More, even, than sex and infidelity.

"What do you mean, Maggie? What can't you beat?"

With this question, the quiet crying broke into gasping sobs. I hugged her for a long couple of minutes, her head on my shoulder. Finally, a few halting words managed to break through from the depths.

"My mom, oh my God, this whole getting old and dying thing. So hard to watch. What could I do? She thanked me. She thanked me. For what? I felt so helpless. So absolutely helpless."

"Maggie, you did what you could. You got the call. You went . . ."

" . . . as soon as I got the call. I sat with her for as long as they let me. I played her music and read her favorite homilies. I put a cool rag to her forehead. But then, I went to rub lotion on her body, so I lifted her gown up, her legs and hips, so thin."

The sobs took over again, as Maggie struggled to get out the words. "There was a huge black and blue mark that started on her thigh and went all the way up to her waist. This huge bruise: it was brand new. I ran to the attendant on duty who explained that despite the rails, mom had squirmed her way off the foot of the bed and crumpled onto the floor. Now they were putting up a rail at the foot of the bed so there's no need for me to worry. No need for me to worry! If only I'd been there . . ."

"But Maggie, even the nurses who are on call 24-7 can't be in the room with her every second. Bad things happen. That doesn't mean you're responsible."

"You don't understand, Carol. It's not just that I wasn't there for my mom. It's that I'm a horrible, horrible human being."

"What are you talking about?"

"The truth is, the whole time I was there, I could only think of one thing. I wanted her to die. It was so hard to see her like that, and with her begging me to get her drugs so she could kill herself. I just wanted it all to end."

I held Maggie in my arms, as she cried uncontrollably. When the sobbing began calming down, I whispered to her, hoping she would take my words to heart.

"Maggie. It doesn't sound like you really wanted your mother to die. Sounds like what you really wanted was to save her from all this, Maggie. Because . . ."

"Because I love my mother so much. And there was nothing I could do to make it all go away."

38

IF ONLY

THE SUN WAS GOING DOWN BEHIND THE Manhattan skyline, the cold light turning incongruously warm and festive shades of pink and orange. Dan would be home soon and Lucky was already positioned at the door.

"You're so lucky you've got Dan," Maggie said, her thoughts finally wrenched away from her mother's bedside, only to settle uncomfortably on her trip back to Los Angeles in the morning, and what awaited her there.

I pulled out some apples and cheese, and refilled Maggie's wine glass with Cabernet. "I thought you and Greg were great together. You obviously love each other," I ventured.

"That's true. But when he lost his job and got so depressed, I suddenly realized that there was nothing more to look forward to. I was never going to get him to move someplace exotic, and I sure as hell didn't want to end up on some remote river somewhere fly-fishing. We were never going to be able to travel the world in the style I'd dreamt about and I was never going to be able to quit my job at the boutique and go back to painting. I was scared that I'd never get to live the life I'd imagined. After all, look at my mom. One day she's taking long walks and fixing us our favorite lasagna. The next day, she's lying in bed babbling old songs about Clementine. Life is so short. You've got to do everything you can to make every moment count. That's what Mexico was about for me."

"So yes, I get it. But if that's true, that you can't travel the world first-class anymore, what is it that you would like?"

Maggie took a sip of her Cabernet, waiting for inspiration. After a long pause, the words came tumbling out.

"I want mom to get better, of course. Although I do know that whatever break we get is only a temporary reprieve. But there's something else. To go back home and not feel like a loser anymore. Greg wants me to grow old with him. He says he loves me, even my imperfections. But I'm afraid. What if I still want more? How do I do that?"

I poured us both a round of Cabernet, and we sat a good, long time in thoughtful silence.

39

SOMETHING

THE SUN WAS NOW COMPLETELY GONE, THE colorful building, street, and rooftop landing lights across the river turning Manhattan into Downtown Disney. Flipping on the houselights, I spotted the Keen book on the entryway table.

"I've been reading this book. I think this guy's got it wired. He says some really smart things."

"Like?"

"That you don't need to know how to make your life meaningful again. You don't need to be good enough. You just need to start somewhere, anywhere, and then keep doing it. You do your part and give the rest to God."

"Lucky for me you don't have to know what you're doing. But it's not easy to start something when you've come to a dead halt. Take you, for instance; what have you started?"

All the self-confidence I had had in my role as confidante and advisor to Maggie suddenly deflated. After all, I was an author of spiritual books who couldn't even find it in herself to pray. But happily, having tapped wells of compassion for my friend, I was gratified to note that I was suddenly also feeling kindly towards myself.

"Truth is, Maggie, I don't know what to make of myself at this point of my life, other than to mourn the passing of old dreams, as well as aspects of my life and identity that I clearly no longer have any control over whatsoever. But I do trust that in time, a new dream will come to me. And I believe the same for you."

"That's something," Maggie said, reaching out to hold my hand.

"Yes," I replied. "That's something."

40

A STRANGE BEING

AFTER MAGGIE LEFT, I BASKED FOR A luxuriously long while in the afterglow of her visit, remembering why it had been that she and I had bonded from the first, and why we had stayed such good friends. We were fearless with one another, and even though we were once again going to be thousands of miles apart, it was great to be the kind of friends who accepted each other unconditionally. But self-acceptance: that was another matter.

I couldn't wait to pick up Sam Keen again. I was hungry to absorb the secret to his unequivocal surrender not to what is possible, but rather, to what one already is. I read him in awe.

"Much of the turmoil of my life has come from struggling to actualize some fantasy or realize an ideal of self that is unfitting. I would like to be happy-go-lucky, leisurely, of lighter spirit. I fool myself into wishing I were somebody totally different from who I actually am. I am unhappy because I am burdened by the demon of philosophy, cursed always to be asking 'why,' an obsessive worker at the meaning game.

"But then in an instant, my perspectives shift, and I accept what before was problematic. I view my history, my parents, my body type, my strange appetite for asking questions, and my

CAROL ORSBORN

unsettled and unsettling mind as my destiny. What was a wound is transformed into a gift. In that moment I know that my ultimate freedom lies in surrendering to this strange being who bears the name Sam Keen."

While Gershon Winkler transcends the questions and turned his back on his life, there is no escape for Sam—only a plunging in. I get it.

It bears repeating: "I know that my ultimate freedom lies in surrendering to this strange being who bears the name Sam Keen," he writes.

I, too, am ready to surrender to this being who bears the name Sam Keen. But I am not so certain that I am either ready, willing, or capable of surrendering to this equally strange and flawed being who bears the name Carol Orsborn.

41

SLIPPING DOWN
THE PYRAMID

UNTIL THIS ENTRY, I HAVE HAD THE LUXURY OF contemplating the interplay between freedom and aging in the context of Dan's continuing to make a steady salary. It is, after all, a gift to have sufficient psychic space to invest in thinking about the meaning of life, rather than how we're going to keep up with our obligations. Not to be overly dramatic, we'll have food on the table no matter what. And for this, I am grateful. But we can't afford a repeat of the kind of winter holiday we enjoyed just a few months ago. We'd flown our daughter, Jody, in from London, and our son, Grant, and his family drove up from Tennessee. Between us, there were three generations and just as many dogs. Because our apartment is small, we'd sublet Claire's place, who had driven off with Daisy to her parents' home in New Jersey for the holidays.

If at least one of us isn't making real money come next Christmas, I imagine that instead of basking side by side in the warmth of a blazing log, we may be huddling separately before the electronic glow of Skype. Instead of new designer coats from Bloomingdale's, it could well be mittens sent via UPS ground.

I suppose it's to be expected that given Dan's patient and generous audience to my ongoing monologue about freedom and choice, it wouldn't be long before the spark of independence lit a fire in his belly. In fact, more and more often, my monologue is being interrupted by Dan inserting little worrisome asides, like, "I miss the freedom of consulting" and "Remember how great it was when we both worked from home in California?"

True, there was an incredibly satisfying decade, just past, in which we both had desks in separate corners of our little cottage in L.A. Lucky loves our canyon home, now rented out to tenants. She puts her paws up at the front window and greets every passerby, many with child or dog in tow.

Then, alas, health-care reform started sputtering. We got notice of a serious raise in our insurance that would have put our retirement savings in jeopardy. And just around the same time, Dan got a call recruiting him for the job in New York— with full benefits. He flew out for the interview, got the nod, and I was left with the sad task of letting our neighbors and their dogs in on the news. "We'll be back," we promised. This, after all, was the house I'd always dreamt about retiring in. But honestly, I never thought it would be quite this soon.

Of course, I understand that Dan has the right to want to choose the nature of his relationship to aging, success, and ambition, as well. I'm not sure why it hadn't occurred to me that Dan, too, would be yearning for freedom. Have I been in denial? Perhaps. I had simply been unwilling to deal with the very real possibility that Dan would willingly—enthusiastically, actually—seriously consider stepping away from the big corporate position that has been underwriting the vision of the genteel, self-chosen version of "financial independence" with which I have been dallying.

42

THE DANCE

WHEN WE WERE YOUNGER WITH A WHOLE life ahead of us and children for whom we were responsible, Dan and I had no choice but to dance with jobs, clients, and bosses who did not always have our best interests at heart. We learned to protect our toes by calling upon reserves of self-discipline and spiritual resources, deriving seemingly boundless energy from sublimated fear and anger. We persevered through the building years, and kept our credit in good enough shape to survive the waves of downturns and recessions that have eroded the shores of our generation's hopes for a cushy retirement. We had finally gotten to a place in our life where we could actually visualize living the dream. Then wham. The raise in our health insurance. Job offer. New York. Holding companies. Stock market crash. Layoffs. Increased pressure. Executive huddles. More cutbacks.

The truth is, neither of us have the stomach for it anymore. Our best hope is to take off our dancing shoes and tiptoe quietly away. But away to where? This is a good question, one I have been thinking much more about than I've let on. Someplace simple and green. Doesn't need to be big. It has a porch. And a Dutch door. Dan and I are there. And so is Lucky.

SPRING

*Life moves upward
and lets the mistakes
sink down behind it.*

—The I Ching

43

THE LAST CAPPUCCINO

IS IT POSSIBLE THAT IT IS ONLY ONE MONTH SINCE I last wrote? How to catch up on what has transpired. . . I will start with today's breakfast. Easter. 8:30 A.M. Awoke to a seriously warm morning after the latest in a series of false starts to a sputtering New York City spring. Strolling with Dan and Lucky to an always crowded little café, hoping that the line won't be too long at the walk-up window where we sometimes treat ourselves to Paris-style cappuccino and croissants. Did I mention that this café is right across from McCarren Park, and the jonquils and tulips are in bloom?

We walk to a park bench where Lucky is positioned to watch the squirrels, her excitement building knowing that we have a pact. When the last bit of our Parisian breakfast is consumed, she will be flying towards the trees doing her favorite thing in the world: making squirrels disappear into the branches. The coffee is thick and rich as melted chocolate, but with a taste sweetened by cream and burn instead of sugar. The cream has been deftly poured into the shape of a steaming heart. It's not cheap. And this morning, when we feel doubly fortunate that there is not only not a long line, but no line at all, Dan and I share a toast to being the richest people on earth.

I let myself spend the money not only because it's Easter, but because I am grabbing many things and experiences for what I believe to be the last time, on our way down.

Here's the thing. Dan was called to his boss's office and asked "How do you think things are going?" Dan told the truth. "I miss consulting." Now we've got three months of severance to figure out what's next. And as I dip my tongue into the more-precious-than-ever steaming cream heart, I think to myself: "If I have to swap this for Dan's happiness, it's a fair trade."

44

REVISED NUMBERS

IT HELPS THAT SINCE I LAST WROTE, I REVISED our income numbers downward to accommodate Dan's startup and had an emergency summit with our financial advisor to come up with a new budget and projection. Turns out the borderline is more malleable than I'd feared. If we cut our expenses exactly in half, continue to produce at least some level of income until age seventy-three, and don't lose anything more on our investments, we should have enough to make it through age eighty-nine, the number I'd made up a couple of months ago. If we can do all that, we can even afford to move back to our cottage in Los Angeles when our tenants move out in December.

While our advisor assures us that this calculation factors in some degree of inflation, as well as fluctuations in our investments, I know that his comforting words may well be little more than wishful fiction. We think we can live on half. We think we can supplement it with at least some income. We think we won't have big surprise expenses. We think FDIC won't collapse and that our age group will be more or less protected from the coming changes in Medicare and Social Security. Fool's gold—but good enough for me to revel in the fact that when Dan wakes up in the morning, he springs rather than drags out of bed.

He is working on his new Web site. If he lands some big clients quickly, this will not have been our last top-of-the-line cappuccino, after all. But come what may, at least we've got this one under our belts, as nothing clears the head more than something as definitive as a designer coffee in the park, especially if it is your last.

45

CLARITY

DAN IS REACHING OUT TO PROSPECTIVE CLIENTS. They're happy to hear from him, and there are promising things in the pipeline. He got the first rejection, as well, denting if not damaging his spirits. But it's a worrisome one. A company that really wants to hire him but is making cuts across the board because this year is turning out to be tighter than expected. Any firm that depends at least in part on government money is in trouble, as talk of debt ceilings and cutbacks fill the headline news. Also in the news: how hard it is for people fifty, let alone sixty-plus, to land a new position once they've been let go.

It's been a tough year for seniority—for those of us who have progressed up the ladder to the point that our value to the mainstream is primarily in the accumulated wealth of our lifetime of knowledge and wisdom. As much as companies would like to gobble us whole to know what we know, they are investing, rather, in fresh young talent. These new recruits don't know beans, but can be relied upon to keep pushing the old rock up the hill at pennies on the dollar.

Like Dan, I have prospects and networking opportunities that I have been scraping together. I have managed to maintain just enough of a presence to preserve my status as a leading marketing expert in a field that few companies care about: older women. At a conference about marketing to women I attended a few months back, where I was representing my Web site client only because the avatar is not real, I was seated next to the thirtyish marketing director of a leading Web site for medical information. She admitted, under cross-examination, that women fifty-plus were not only their largest segment, but the fastest-growing, as well. All her marketing dollars were going, however, towards Gens X and Y.

"Why?" I asked.

"Because there's no future in investing in Boomer women."

"You mean, because we're going to die?"

"Well, if you want to put it that way," she replied, "yes."

"But the average Boomer woman has three decades ahead of her, while statistically, your job is unlikely to exceed 18 months."

This conversation ended abruptly as she got up to leave the table for something suddenly more pressing.

I sat for too long a time at the table, an island of age with empty chairs to the left and right. Scanning the crowd, a wave of astonishment bowled me over. How could this be? When did this happen?

I was the oldest person in the room.

46

THE PROMISED LAND

EVER SINCE I STUMBLED ACROSS A BURNING bush at summer camp when I was an impressionable kid, I have identified with Moses. No miracle, the bush was merely part of a controlled burn. And admittedly, I am "no Moses," either. But I have nevertheless always taken comfort and inspiration from the story of his struggles to live up to God's expectations. I especially like the part about Moses stuttering, and having to inspire his people, anyway.

In my own, lesser way I have felt called by God to take on the prophetic role of challenging the old constricting stereotypes and beliefs about aging. As the marketing to women conference reminded me, this is not always the easiest path to walk. Like Moses, I have often felt unqualified and unworthy . . . and yet I persist.

While I take my inspiration from Moses, I do so with trepidation. For the concluding chapters of his story have always troubled me. Why would God have forbidden Moses at the end of his life from entering the Holy Land for one tiny act of disobedience—not even consciously intended?

What did Moses do, exactly? He smote a rock with a stick in order to bring water forth to sustain his followers who were dying of thirst. He saved their lives. However, God, it seems, would have preferred Moses not to smite but rather to speak to the rock to obtain his result. And for this act of self-will, Moses is rebuked: "Because ye believed not in Me, to sanctify Me in the eyes of the children of Israel, therefore ye shall not bring this assembly into the land which I have given them."

This seems to be a huge punishment for smiting instead of speaking.

Surely, I have been even more disobedient than Moses over the course of my life, despite good intentions. As I look towards the Promised Land I'm hoping is to be found somewhere on this side of sixty, I wonder if I, too, will be denied a happy ending to my story.

47

SMOTE

I HAVE SUSPECTED FOR SOME TIME NOW THAT what I have meant when I said I was searching for freedom was actually the falling away of the false, and the expansion of life into what is true. It is truth that opens up the opportunity for meaning, providing us with the fullest spectrum of possibilities in regards to fulfilling the authentic human potential. For what other purpose would freedom be worthwhile?

But with age, is it possible for truth tellers to become too undiluted for human consumption? I thought back with a strange mixture of pride and discomfort over the confrontation of my recent table companion, the young medical Web site marketer who thought it was a waste of time to target older women. Perhaps we reach a point where it is not only prudent, but our duty to step aside so that the wheels of daily life can continue to turn towards the future—not for our own, but for the benefit of generations to come?

This is normally the kind of question I would take to God. Through prayer, meditation, and journaling, I would open myself to divine guidance and listen deeply for direction. I might, for instance, return to the Bible to study a particular passage that has come to mind, seeing in it the wise and loving presence of God speaking directly to my heart. And then, inspired, I would take out my notebook and write a prayer to God. But as I review my account of this year's struggle with aging, it is painfully apparent that God has been a bit player at best, making guest appearances but not pervading my consciousness, even when I was trying my best. Something has been blocking me from connection to the divine that I cannot put my finger on, let alone remedy. As a result, even while bringing everything I possibly can to my effort to hold my own against the onslaught of aging, I have spent so much of this difficult year feeling that in this journey into the unknown, I have been on my own. And no wonder. For as I answer the urge to turn the page to the last episode in the Hebrew Scriptures regarding Moses, I find myself burning with anger.

Where is the God of justice, the God of love, the God of compassion? How could God have meted out such harsh punishment to Moses for what?—for smiting, for God's sake! What kind of God is this? To use Moses like that, to bring him to the brink of deliverance to the Promised Land, and then bar the way. And not only Moses, but all of us. What kind of God asks so much of us decade after decade, to birth our children, to build our lives, to make our contributions to society, and in the end, what? Aging and death.

48

GIVING NOTICE

THE BUILDING HAS BEEN NOTIFIED THAT WE'LL BE moving out as soon as we can find someone to take over our apartment. We are told it won't take long. There is always a fresh class of new recruits to the corporate mainstream flooding into the city. If we do sublet it quickly, that leaves us all summer and fall without a clue as to where we will live, not to mention what we'll be doing to make ends meet when the severance gives out.

We have concerns. Despite the budget projections that conscribe our possibilities, a rotten economy is now the "new normal." In any case, it is unlikely that given our taste for freedom, either of us will ever want to do what it would take to replace our last job's level of security, income, and benefits. The good news is that we are also unlikely to replace the particular level and type of stress that comes coupled with accountability to shareholders. I look at Dan and know that he is confident that we're going to be okay. Some days I am in awe of his level of ease about being in transition. Other days, I think he's just deep in denial.

Regardless, even as the sand trickles through the hourglass, Dan wakes up singing, rejoicing that he doesn't have to rush to the subway for work, while I have been halfheartedly kicking my splayed donkey of a career back towards the fast track to save the day. No matter that my work life is sprawled out on the ground, tongue out and panting, collapsed under the burden of old age. Nevertheless, I find myself pushing myself to make another call, take one more lunch, put out a dozen more e-mails before I remember that oh, yes: I'm not who I used to be.

49

PINCH MY THIGH

I HAVE BEEN BEGGING FOR FREEDOM—AND HERE IT is. Nobody is taking me up on my offers to be of service. There are no demands being put upon me. Dan has taken to singing Janis Joplin: "Freedom's just another word for nothing left to lose." Only occasionally do I remember to laugh with him.

For me, there's something strangely askew with this picture. For I have always thought of freedom as being whole and complete unto itself. It is true that delivered to this side of the illusions of the omnipotence of youth, freedom has given me the gift of no longer wasting valuable energy on those who don't fully appreciate what I have to offer. Untethered from the past, freedom is leaving behind old beliefs, behaviors, and relationships that I have outgrown. There is freedom, too, in the expression of my authentic thoughts and feelings without preamble, explanation, or apology. And yet, I cannot deny that this freedom is missing something central, critical, urgent. This freedom is missing me.

Not exactly "me," for somebody is sitting here and scribbling out this diary. When I pinch my thigh, "I" still feel it. The green cargo pants I'm wearing are the same pants I wore a couple of years ago, when I was still "myself."

But as I begin putting books back into the box for the move, I notice that whole chunks of my life that were just a few years ago critical to the sense of who I am are now going into the crate marked *Salvation Army*. A red book about management, a green one about menopause, and blue books about dieting, entertaining, and parenting. I'm keeping the pastel-colored books on spirituality and the yellow and black guides to financial planning and retirement, even though I've read them through from cover to cover.

As I sort, I am studying myself making choices, looking for clues about myself. Reaching the bottom of the stack, I am about to give up hope of illumination when my hands connect with a forgotten book, consistently ignored and overlooked, that is not just whispering but crying out to me: "Yes, yes, yes! You're finally ready. We've been waiting for you!"

50

THE CLUE

THIS LAST BOOK IS A VIRGIN. PRISTINE. THERE are no underlines, no highlights, no notes in the margins because after I purchased it two years ago, just after it was published, I hid it.

The handsome trade paperback was written by a woman I respect, a friend even, but I could not even bear to open the front cover after buying it. The book upset me and all I can say for myself is that I had sufficient self-awareness to be ashamed of myself for my resistance to reading it. Now, I grab at it as if it were a lifeline thrown to one who is sinking into the void. The title, alone, holds the promise of salvation: *Who Am I . . . Now That I'm Not Who I Was?*

Five older women call out to me from the cover of author Connie Goldman's book. They are in various states of agedness, grayness, and wrinkledness. Two years ago, I felt sorry for them and their bittersweet question. But suddenly, I wonder, hopefully, what gifts of wisdom these old women have to share. They are not who they used to be, but they look happy, vibrant, alive. I pick up the book and begin reading. I read from Vicki, age sixty-three, to Betty, age eighty-seven, and dozens of stories and ages in between, and my hunch is affirmed. They do, indeed, know things. What they know is this: the challenge that comes bundled with living a long life is "not just to grow old but to grow whole."

Growing whole: this is a glimpse of what I have been missing—the essence that has previously eluded me. And no wonder, I've been going about it exactly backwards. All my life I've been so adept at making things happen. Doesn't it make sense that if something's missing, you add something on? Life isn't going the way you want it—do something about it. Work harder or longer, make and keep a budget, network with your friends, and if that doesn't work, take up yoga and start eating tofu. Still missing something? Sign up for a meditation retreat or make a deal with God about how hard you're going to pray.

But here, on the wild side of sixty, I am ready to be initiated into the deeper mysteries, realizing that this wholeness for which I yearn—the radical freedom and self-acceptance modeled by Connie and the women in her book—is not something I could ever make happen. Suddenly, it is so painfully obvious. Of course! Becoming whole comes about not from an adding on, but rather, from a stripping away. We are to let go of the parts of ourselves we've assembled out of leftovers and scotch tape, having covered over our authentic selves with roles and responses that, if we are lucky and courageous, we eventually outgrow. We chose our careers because we were afraid we couldn't get paid for what we really love to do. We dyed our hair to keep our jobs. Some have suffered through loveless marriages for the sake of the children and most put our own needs and desires so far on the back burner, we don't even remember when the water boiled away.

But then, given the gift of a long enough life, so much of what we once thought was central to our survival and identity drops away. Daring to turn my gaze toward the heart of the mystery, I get a glimpse of a very old woman on a park bench. I have passed her by many times, but I have never stopped to really look at her. She is alone. She is quiet. I am inclined to feel sorry for her, knowing how much she has left behind only to have arrived on this bench in a park, nothing more for her to do. But this time, I see something I have never stopped to notice before. She is smiling.

51

STRIPPED

THIS STRIPPING AWAY OF WHO I USED TO BE TURNS out not to be only the bad thing I fear. What if it were in fact the key to everything I've always wanted? At last, I am getting a glimpse of what freedom might look like for me. The shedding of others' impositions is no less than the simultaneous reclamation of pieces of myself previously dealt away to others. In the words of Florida Scott-Maxwell: "If at the end of your life you have only yourself, it is much. Look and you will find."

But where to begin? The list of impositions goes back a long way. When I was born, my mother, Mae, already had a son, the first boy child in a culture that privileges firstborn males. They were cut from the same cloth, mother and son, with cool personalities that preferred to judge than to hug. Mae was the iron maiden and her minion was the prince, heir to both personality and domain. And this cool intimacy was amplified by the absence of Mae's husband, off to the battlefields of World War II. He did not meet his son until the child was five years old. That was the same year, nine months later, that I was born.

Lloyd came home from war, as much an outsider as I to the bond between mother and son. He yearned for an offspring more in his own style of ebullient warmth. From the first moment he laid eyes on me, I was Daddy's little girl. This, it turns out, was a mixed blessing. For in our family, from as early as I can remember, we had to choose sides. I am a slow learner—or an eternal optimist—but I never stopped trading pieces of myself away in hopes of winning my mother's love, too.

THE PORTRAIT

I REMEMBER THE ACTUAL MOMENT WHEN I FELL from grace and began doling pieces of myself away to others.

I was age four when a photographer had been invited to the house to do a portrait sitting of mother and daughter. My mother had dressed me in the latest fashion, hoping that this would reflect positively on her. The photographer, a pinched middle-aged man in suit and hat, took one look at the toddler, a vibrant, grinning beam of light, turned to Mae, and pronounced: "What a fat little girl."

While I may not have understood the literal meaning of such a judgment, I could clearly see that the last glimmer of hope had died in my mother's eyes. I was never going to be the daughter my mother wanted—the one whose being affirmed her essence.

Having failed to win her love through the mere fact of my existence, I learned early on that the only way I could get my mother's attention was by regaling her with bright and shiny stories about my accomplishments. I was working up a frenzy spinning tales to earn a place in the family, while my brother—private and cool—got a free ride.

It wasn't long before I turned myself into a super-achiever, winning attention often at my own expense. Even years later, as I grew into a published author, I would sit down at the computer in the early morning and write nonstop until late at night, not changing from my pajamas, not taking breaks for food or even to go to the bathroom.

When my publisher put me on tour, I traveled to a city a day, doing back-to-back interviews to the point that I sometimes passed out from exhaustion. I never said a word to protect myself. In fact, there were many years in which if I weren't depleted to the point of feeling ill, I felt I wasn't doing enough.

53

THE LAST TIME

I NEVER GAVE UP HOPE FOR A BETTER-LATE-than-never core recognition of my essential worthiness. During my father's prolonged death, I bit my tongue every time Mother asked when my brother was going to stop by, as I watched the red roses he brought for a visit late in the course of my father's life turn black in the vase, mother refusing to let them go.

My brother and I got the call at the same time. Dad had passed. But, driving faster, my brother was already seated in the living room with Mae when I arrived. They were making small talk, as if my father weren't lying so newly dead in the bedroom. Mother rose to meet me at the door and whispered in my ear: "Please don't make a scene. Your brother doesn't like emotion."

I rushed through the living room into the bedroom, where my father lay, his inert hand still clenching the bars of his rented hospital bed. I threw myself against the railing, clasping his fingers with my own, sobbing out of control as I kissed my father's hand for the last time. At that moment, I made a vow.

I vowed that the admonition that I veil my emotions so as

not to upset my brother was to be the final pillaging of my sacred sanctorum by a family member, or anybody, for that matter. There would never again be the suffering of teachers who judged too harshly, bosses who took too much credit and employees who took too much advantage. This inviolable boundary would apply to neighbors, friends, receptionists at spas, and all those to whom I had given away essential pieces of myself that I now feel it critical to retrieve.

54

RECKONING

OF COURSE, IN THE SUDDEN FLOW OF MEMORIES pouring into my diary, I am forced to confront the fact that when it comes to the violation of boundaries, I have not always been the victim. I may vow to never allow my essence to be trespassed again. But must I also vow never to transgress another's? And where I have been making some progress at forgiving others, have I even begun the process of forgiving myself?

Oh yes, I have my own amends to make, as I weigh and balance my own yearnings to control and protect those for whom I care so profoundly with the urge to empower and set free. Just as I struggled against the repressive dynamics of my family of origin, as my own children have grown into adulthood, I have suffered mightily as each has found ways to struggle within, against, and finally break out to make sacred vows of their own.

This should be cause for rejoicing, but there has also been pain. I understand all too well the context for their complaints, feeling both guilt and responsibility. But at the same time, there is the growing awareness that even a flawed, responsible, and guilty parent has the right to set boundaries.

55

MEA STILL CULPA

YES, I HAVE FORGIVEN MUCH. BUT STILL, NOT SO quickly. I have not yet even touched upon the greatest guilt I feel: my failure to stand firm behind what I have seen as my most sacred trust. This is no less than the conviction that our children have the God-given right to live out their dreams as visionaries, artists, and people who deserve abundant love, hope, and balance. On one hand, did I ill-prepare my children for a world that is increasingly limited, with fewer opportunities to break through barriers? Life is hard under the best of circumstances. But to have encouraged my children to become musicians, scholars, writers, entrepreneurs: to follow their hearts when I should have known the odds were stacked against them?

Now, washed up on the shore of my own later-in-life limitations, I am quite frankly rethinking my lifetime investment in the notion that one could have a significant positive impact on how things turn out in the end. As I watch my children believing in the attainability of a meaningful life, I not only have doubts about the quality of my convictions, but regret and anger about an unforgiving world.

On the other hand, I understand, now, the prophetic nature of my vision—that trying to break free from a corrupt status quo is a high-risk mission. Surely there are safer lives, and certainly it would be easier for one to give up hope than to try to be an alive, healthy person in the midst of dissolution. If I had to do it all over again, I'm pretty sure I would still err on the side of encouraging others to do everything within their power to make this round of life count to the fullest, regardless of the risk. What else could life possibly be for?

56

STORM WARNINGS

THE KEG GUY AND I ARRIVED AT CLAIRE'S apartment at the same moment, both Daisy and Lucky jumping up crazy-eyed with excitement. There had been quiet murmurings about the neighbors and their dogs throwing us some kind of good-bye party at some point, and out of old habit, I wondered if we were to at last be included on a guest list. But in my heart of hearts, I was 100 percent certain that whatever plans they were cooking up for us wouldn't center on anything as cool as cracking open a keg of beer. Tea, maybe, or Cabernet. Anyway, Dan was away, a scouting trip to Chicago in hopes of landing a client for his new consulting practice.

The news was full of warnings about a big storm moving in, so Lucky, Daisy, and I got our late afternoon round of squirrel hunting in earlier than usual. Once I'd returned Daisy safely home, making sure she had plenty of water in her dish, I put the whole party thing out of my mind. There was plenty to do. With Dan out of the house, I could make any kind of a mess I wanted, sorting through the papers, knickknacks, and stacks of clothes that had accumulated over the course of the year. There were three piles: keep was on the bed, giveaway in the front hallway, and throwaway on the kitchen floor.

Television weather played subliminally in the background, lest I miss the warning of a repeat of last fall's tornado. Dan had called to remind me to bring the cushions, the watering can, and plants inside before the lightning, thunder, and driving rain came crashing down. We signed off with our ritual litany of kisses, love ya's, and miss you's, supplemented by Dan's heartfelt admonition to keep Lucky and me safe and dry. I thought of poor Lucky during the last tornado, knee-deep in hail, and shuddered. How courageous and foolhardy she was to plummet headfirst into the storm in search of something as elusive as a squirrel, as if a squirrel would ever have made it to a seventh floor deck. She must have been terrified by the fierce wind pinning her to the door. And, too, I thought of how reckless I was to have allowed that to happen in the first place.

How much life asks of us—and how vigilant we must be, especially on the wild side of midlife. The line between life and death had grown very thin, indeed—and in less time than it had taken for something as simple and inconsequential as a door to crack the littlest bit open. While the sky continued darkening, as I sorted out the last piece of clothing, heated up a can of Campbell's soup for dinner, settled down to sip, and watched the news, I could not put Lucky down. And so it was, her warm, little body tucked on my lap, first she and then I drifted off into a light doze.

57

STILL . . .

A KNOCK ON THE DOOR STARTLED US AWAKE. Lucky scrambled off my lap, piercing the air with hysterical barks. The television screen had started beeping, and in my scrambled mind, I feared that a tornado was once again hard upon us. Focusing my eyes, the dark sky seemed eerily still, but I soon realized that the beeps were warning only of an impending lightning storm, nary a twister in site. Another knock impelled me off the sofa to grab Lucky up and answer the door.

"Hi. Sorry to disturb you. But do you know Claire?" Standing before me was a handsome man, George Clooney around the eyes with splashes of Hugh Grant around the lips and chin. "My cousin's having a party, and I've misplaced her apartment number. All I remembered was seventh floor."

"Sure. I know Claire. And Daisy."

"Oh yes, Daisy. World's most terrifying pit bull." We laughed lightly, Lucky trading her protective growls for affectionate sniffs. I put Lucky down and the man reached down to pat her on the head. Dancing up on her hind legs, Lucky responded with a flurry of unbridled licks. "You live here?" he asked. I positioned myself to block the view of cushions and messy piles scattered all over the apartment, but he was looking past all that towards the wall of dark glass that lit up occasionally with distant bolts of lightning. "Storm coming," he pronounced, pointing towards the deck. "I bet this is a great view. I'd love to take a peek."

He seemed in no hurry to leave, an intuition that was quickly affirmed. "My name's Justin, by the way. Claire's older cousin. Oh, I already said that. I can't believe I agreed to come to her party. I thought I'd been to my last keg party years ago—nice chilled Chablis is much more my style."

One intuition following hard upon the other, my rusty gears slowly began to turn. Was this grown man—this Justin—flirting with me? I thought instantaneously of Maggie, cringing at the memory of how I'd not only felt superior to her affair with Webster, but—dare I admit it—jealous? No, not really jealous of the affair. But of her reprieve from growing old, to have turned the clock back to once again be seen, to be visible, to be desired.

"Lucky, leave Justin alone!" I peeled Lucky tongue-first off of Justin, then followed quickly with an offer to walk him to Claire's apartment.

"I'm in no hurry," he answered. To which I replied: "Would you like to see the view?"

58

JUST TALKING

WE STOOD AT THE WINDOW, THE DISTANT lightning coming closer with each flash, and talked about a lot of things. I told him about our year in New York, about the books I'd written, and our cottage in Los Angeles. We talked about dogs. Of course, I left a lot of things out, especially anything having to do with the main thing that had preoccupied my consciousness for most of this year: growing old.

In return, he told me about his career as an architect, which was booming, his midlife crisis, which was raging, and his marriage, which was over. I can't remember everything we talked about, but it didn't matter. It wasn't the words I was paying attention to, anyway. Rather, I was being ravished from the inside out by a bolt of vitality that came to me from out of the distant past. I was not to be held responsible for how I felt. For this was no less than a most unexpected and timely reprieve from what I now understood to have been a premature and unnecessary coming to terms with aging. Instantly once again lithe and sparkling, I deserved this. This was right. This was fair. Thunder, once little more than a subliminal growl, began to build quickly—the intensity duly noted, then suddenly demanding complete and full attention. A roiling, a rumbling, a clap, an explosion, and a knock, a knock, and another knock. A quick glance, guilty awareness breaking in on us both. Somebody was at the door.

"There you are, Justin!" It was Claire. "Charles said he saw you getting into the elevator ages ago."

"Hi, Claire. Sorry. We're just finishing. Your neighbor and I got to talking and the time ran away with me." Justin turned back to me, offered me a tender salute, and whispered: "Thanks."

"Thanks?" The instant this word issued from my lips, I regretted it. It was certainly not a question that wanted, let alone begged, for a response. But it got one.

"Thanks for listening, I mean. You see, you remind me so much of my mother," Justin proclaimed. "Doesn't she, Claire, remind you of Mom?" Then turning back to me: "Hey, you should come to the party. Claire, is it okay if I invite your neighbor?" Then turning back to me. "You drink beer?"

Do I drink beer? Boston Lager: clear and deep amber with a malty sweetness; Negra Modela or Dos Equis, rich, smooth, and dark; German Hefewiezen, thick and golden, Guinness, heavy and foamy white, Dan's favorite. Our first trip to Europe, Dan and I swinging giant mugs to the beat of the accordion, Grant at five years old, running through the beer hall in Munich under the lights and stars. Jody's graduation trip to London, the barkeep writing her name in foam while Dan, Grant, and I all laughed together in collusion, that at only eighteen she was considered old enough to drink. An ice chest full of beer cans and bottles: Grant and Ginny's rehearsal dinner on a pool patio in St. Thomas, raising our glasses high to the bride and groom, drinking deeply of life and toasting the past, present, and future with a taste on my lips as exquisitely bittersweet as hops. I struggled to hold back tears now, so humiliated and ashamed of how readily in the moment I'd forgotten who I was—all the richness of my long, precious life. And for what? At the first opportunity, my ego had taken a joyride into a fantasy born out of the misguided belief that I'd been granted a reprieve from aging. His mother? When my ego crashed, it took a year of hard-won spiritual progress with it. No, it was worse than that. I could see now, despite my repeated attempts to pray, my contemplative reading, my moments of insight, there had been no spiritual progress whatsoever. Nothing had stuck. I had been fooling myself that I had won even one inch of ground in my struggle to wrest meaning out of life at this daunting new age and stage of my life. It had all been smoke and mirrors, just as I'd mistaken Justin's nostalgia for his mother for flirting.

"No," I replied to Justin, then, turning to Claire, "But would it be possible for you to take Lucky for the night? There's something I must do."

"No problem. We'll take good care of her." And all three were gone, leaving me alone with my foolishness.

59

THE SHALLOWS

THAT'S NOT EXACTLY TRUE. I WASN'T ENTIRELY alone. Sam Keen, Gershon Winkler, Connie, Maggie, the old woman on the park bench: they had all risen from the pages of my precious books and diaries to mock me, the persistence of my illusions and the shallowness of my faith. A lifetime of spiritual pursuit: wasted. All of it: little more than fairy tales and self-medication. I, who had believed myself to have come so far, was reconciled with absolutely nothing.

A fat, ragged bolt of lightning, traveling a path so close it raised the hair on the back of my neck, was closely followed by a thunderous crash so loud I put my hands over my ears and screamed. And in that second, before I could stop myself, I threw open wide the door to the deck and dashed outside. I raised my fist into the driving rain, crying out into the stormy night: "You want me so freaking bad, God? Then take it all. Take my vanity, my arrogance, my foolishness, take everything I am and do with me what you will."

Another bolt and deafening crash, no longer separated by even a gasp. The metal fence in the park across the street shot off sparks into the night sky. A howling gale screamed into my ears but I screamed louder: "I'm done trying and I refuse to go on like this, afraid and humiliated. So what are you waiting for? Come and get me. If this is all that's left, only pain and loss and fear and regret, then take me. Take me now!"

Once more lightning and thunder struck. Seven stories below, a tree burst into flame, the acrid smoke of electricity and wood instantaneously rising to my nose on the wind. And just then, when by all reason, I was in the direct path destined to get hit next, there came, instead, a small, still voice.

"This is not surrender, Carol. This is not even acceptance. This is just plain stupid! Standing in the middle of a lightning storm, daring Me to take you on your terms. When are you going to get that this is simply not your show! None of it. You don't want to be afraid anymore? You don't want to make humiliating mistakes? You don't want to get old and die someday? What makes you so freaking special? Now get out of this storm and dry yourself off. The last thing any of us wants is for your keyboard to electrocute you."

"Keyboard?"

"Yes. Go inside now, and write."

"Write what?"

The answer was a blinding flash of light so close, I did not stop to argue. Running for my life, I slammed the door behind me, dried my hands, and started to type. As if taking dictation, my screen began filling with words.

60

SPIRITUAL TRUTHS

I DON'T KNOW IF I SAT THERE TYPING FOR minutes or for hours, but somewhere in the midst of suspended time, the storm passed, and a beam of light appeared, reflecting brightly off my screen. It was the moon, come to light up the dark night through the rapidly dispersing clouds. The sight caught me by surprise, and I started to weep. These weren't tears of sorrow. No, these were tears of gratitude. I had been spared, at least for tonight. But I now understood, not just intellectually nor even just emotionally, but in the very depths of my mortal soul, that it was not only my destiny but also everybody else's to die someday. I would not, could not, make peace with aging until I had come to terms with the finitude of existence, including the possibility of suffering and the guarantee of death, none of which were likely to be on my own terms.

But there was something more, something essential. Hope. Hope cultivated in the midst of life's messiness, growing old, and all that implies. Death, I was coming to realize, is not the ultimate violation of our boundaries, to be defied with anger or self-hatred. What, then, is it? You have but two choices: ask yourself if you put your faith in God—or if you do not. I still do not understand why we all have to die but in the flash of the final lightning bolt, running for my life, I understood something that made all the difference. Death was at the very least not intended by God as punishment. How much time had I invested worrying that I hadn't lived up to expectations, that it was too late to make amends? How much precious time spent worrying about what was to become of me?

Instinctively, I turned to the computer screen, believing that the words I had taken down held the key to all I'd been seeking this long, hard year—and in fact, my entire life. And so it was that, illuminated by the light of the moon, I read through "The 11 Spiritual Truths of Aging."

THE 11 SPIRITUAL TRUTHS OF AGING

1

The less of whom we think we used to be, the
more room there is for God.

2

Others' rejection is our freedom.

3

When we are doing God's work, we are not the
judge of our success.

4

Regret is God calling us to forgive more and
love with fewer conditions.

5

We can dance with rather than struggle against
the essence of who we are.

6

The gift of longevity provides ample opportunity
to not only grow old, but to grow whole.

7

When confronted with ultimate concerns, we can
be more curious than afraid.

8

We have never been better equipped than we are
now to face life as it arises.

9

Ultimately, hope is more important than peace.

10

We don't always get to take a leap of faith.
Sometimes, we are pushed.

11

(more to come)

61

QUIETNESS

AS I THINK ABOUT THE ENTIRETY OF MY LIFE, there are points of time upon which my destiny has pivoted. Leaving home to go to college, marrying Dan, the births of my children and grandchild, the breast cancer diagnosis and recovery, the donning of my doctoral robes, the passing of each of my parents: every one of these both definitively ended and initiated a chapter of my life. Who I was before each of these life-changing events, while bearing the hallmarks of what was to come, could predict neither the surprise nor the inevitability of what it meant to become more fully myself. Now I was to add my encounter with God in the midst of a lightning storm on a penthouse deck as the latest page in my book of life. I didn't know the title of this chapter yet, let alone how it would play out over the years. Would I live long or short? Would I ever truly feel I'd fulfilled my life purpose? Would I die with regret or in peace? All I knew for sure was that something profound in the depths of my soul had shifted in the midst of the storm, and that whatever it was that had transpired was both important and deeply, irrevocably good. Life is mysterious, awe-some and awe-ful, all at once. Can we be wise enough to embrace it all? Happily, I had no doubts. It's never too late.

As the beam of moonlight traveled across the room, my eyes followed it to a single piece of paper tucked into one of the sacred texts on my altar. It was a poem by Rumi.

Quietness

Inside this new love, die.
Your way begins on the other side.
Become the sky.
Take an axe to the prison wall.
Escape.
Walk out like someone suddenly born into color.
Do it now.
You're covered with thick cloud.
Slide out the side. Die,
and be quiet. Quietness is the surest sign
that you've died.
Your old life was a frantic running
from silence.

The speechless full moon
comes out now.

62

THE COST OF DENIAL

FOR AS MANY MONTHS AS I CAN REMEMBER, I'D been wandering through a spiritual desert. There was my self-righteous anger, my vanity, my whining, and my self-pity. My jealousy of those who had not yet been spit out of their old roles and of those who had returned for a repeat performance, however sordid or brief. Then, too, there was the lack of courage with which to name my hopelessness. My own ingrained fears and prejudices about the aged.

I said earlier that I do not only want to grow older; like Sam Keen and Connie Goldman and all the other mentors I have encountered over the course of this year, I also fiercely want to grow more whole. But until my night in the lightning storm, I hadn't fully understood what this would entail. For when integrity includes the confrontation and embrace of one's own dark side—including the shadows of mortality—and views with disdain the centrality of one's own pathos, this is also the willing ascent to despair.

If this is the key to accepting age as it truly is, neither romanticizing nor reviling growing old, no wonder so many of us prefer the relative comfort of denial. Given my history of breast cancer coupled with the one-by-one deaths of both Dan's and my parents, I thought I'd made peace with mortality long ago. Apparently not, or at the very least, not to the degree of acceptance I'd hoped to have achieved by now. This is not necessarily a bad thing. As it turns out, a certain degree of denial is life-affirming. We do not, God forbid, want to live our lives in gothic morbidity. In fact, we not only want, but need to be able to call upon the comfort of living in the present moment, inspired forward to get up and go to work or make dinner for a friend or even, yes, find the strength and courage to take a dog squirrel hunting. But understand this, too. It is dangerous to us, both individually and as a generation, to confuse denial with any kind of shortcut to serenity, let alone the truth.

There is proof enough that ultimately, over-reliance upon denial enslaves us to become victims to the passing of time. Trapped, we find ourselves flailing at the surface of things, unwittingly whipped here and there by the deeper currents we do not even know have us in their grip.

The evidence is everywhere. You name it. Few in our generation are ready for it. Expecting to reap the rewards of the longevity bonus, we are a generation who has had better health and education than any cohort of adults in history. Yet raised in an ageist society that reveres youth and reviles age, we have been complicit in allowing denial to catch us unprepared. Too many of us trusted financial planners we shouldn't have while neglecting to heed the warnings about the cost of long-term care. In search of eternal youth, we bought the expensive anti-aging cream and underwent the elected pain of the knife.

As a cohort with a history of righting injustice, we have yet to grapple adequately with the economic challenges facing our country, to do everything within our power to ensure that not only we but our children will have a safety net to rely upon. Some of us have been foolishly counting on raking in big salaries forever, others are kidding ourselves with the hope that our children will be both able and willing to take care of us.

And, too, don't we all know someone who hasn't wanted to deal with the possibility that down the road she might develop hip or leg issues that will make her a prisoner of the second floor retirement dream condo she just sank her life savings into? And what about those amongst us who have thrown ourselves into second or third careers, who climb mountains and push ourselves beyond endurance without ever stopping to ask whether we are being driven by passion or by fear?

It is not a pretty thing to watch when one by one, myself, my friends, and associates are jolted awake by circumstances beyond our control. There is a price to be paid not only for having turned our backs on ultimate concerns, but also for the contingent avoidance of psychological, spiritual, and practical preparation for our inevitable confrontation with the frailty of the illusions in which we are so invested. When we do wake up, we are overcome with paralyzing anxiety about nearly everything.

The fact is that we can only be fully alive to the degree to which we are willing to become aware of the enormity of existence. In words inspired by Nietzsche: "To grow wise you must first learn to listen to the wild dogs barking in your cellar."

63

THE OTHER SIDE

ON THE MORNING AFTER THE STORM, LUCKY AND Dan safely returned to my arms, my encounter with God on the penthouse deck felt like a dream. I was afraid that I would forget everything and return to my previous state, doing everything I could to avoid being dragged into my next life stage. But when I looked at my computer screen, there were the Spiritual Truths I had received and I knew that it was real. I could, at last, relax my grip on the wheel of life. In its place, I could relish the possibility of finding myself in unexpected places beyond my own imagining and effort. I could willingly let myself be marched to the edge of human knowledge and personal limitations, looking life in the eye without denial, intensely appreciative and deeply trusting, even as I embraced both the shadows and the light.

As Rumi had instructed me by the light of the moon, I had at last found my way. And no wonder it had taken so long and been so difficult. My way could only begin once I had come to terms with nearly everything I'd ever known to start my life anew on the other side: unmapped territory with few markings, no roads, and only the return of faith in God to light the way.

64

FIERCE WITH REALITY

SO THIS IS HOW FREEDOM ON THE WILD SIDE OF sixty is shaping up. This is a freedom that falls asleep at night feeling that at least today, I have tried my best. Freedom is also giving up worrying about who I used to be. No longer measuring myself according to other's expectations, nor basking in hard-won attention that comes at my own expense. Freedom is becoming increasingly willing to accept that I am imperfect, even at setting boundaries.

Freedom is wanting to be more fully forgiving of my mother, my brother, the kids growing up, and even the avatar who replaced me. I want to be quiet for long periods of time. I want to read and stare out the window and do nothing more than pet Lucky's hair in the direction it naturally falls.

Once again, Florida Scott-Maxwell has insight to describe how I'm feeling:

"You need to claim the events in your life to make yourself yours. When you truly possess all you have been and done, which may take some time, you are fierce with reality."

Does it make sense, after this litany of boundary struggles and violations, for me to say that at this moment, I feel very tender about all my relationships, including my relationship to myself? After all, the transgressions that I both suffered and committed have contributed to the present moment, as I sit here writing in my diary, feeling humbled, grateful, hopeful.

I admit that I have tears rolling down my cheeks, leaving trails of ink on the page. I am not entirely sure if they are the bitter-sweet tears of regret or the tears of unbounded gratitude, and I don't particularly feel the need to sort it out. For it all seems to me, at this moment, that everything I have written about, and everything I feel, constitutes the woof and weave of the fabric of my life. And I am, above all, grateful to be alive.

65

FIERCER STILL

WE HAVE RECEIVED BREATHTAKING NEWS. We have found someone to take over our lease on our apartment in Brooklyn and in one month, we have to be out.

Our penthouse's future is secure, the new young tenant looking as sturdy in his expanding life as we had been when we signed the original lease. He crows at our door, overflowing with the vitality born of early-in-life success, a posture that may last him another thirty or maybe even forty years. He is somebody who has made his fortune in the music business, standing there dealing money to the landlord like cards off a deck. How long will his career last? And even should his livelihood hold steady through the decades into midlife and beyond, what about his beauty, his health, and his certainty that he is the master of life?

Oh . . . these are not pretty emotions, but even on this side of transformation there are cycles of expansion and retraction. It is as if the waves of awakening keep coming in an infinite variety of revelations. But so, too, does each insight recede, leaving but a salty reminder of what had just seconds ago engulfed one's being with its fierce truth. It's not easy to give up who you once were.

Perhaps this explains why during that wild night of typing in the storm, the 11th of the 11 Truths of Aging had been left incomplete, with a vague, parenthetical but promising *"more to come."* Three little words, as tender as a sigh, now served as a placeholder for my humility—a reminder that as far as I'd come, I wasn't through yet. Would the 11th Truth ever be fully revealed to me? And if it were, would it be something I would heartily embrace as a culmination? Or would it be yet another dose of tough love? Of course, I would hope for the best, but my call to action was from this point on to take life—all of it—as it arises. Sometimes, my spirit would soar. Sometimes, it would be embarrassingly clear both to myself and others that aspects of myself I'd hoped to have long ago left behind had come along for the ride.

As my friend Connie says: "Sometimes, it seems like only the good parts have dropped away, and the disliked parts, such as worrying, judgments, and the like are the only parts that remain. But the thing is: the falling away—this is growth, too."

66

120 YEARS OLD

LIKE MOTH TO FLAME, I FIND MYSELF ONCE AGAIN drawn to the story of Moses at the end of his life. But this time, after the lightning storm, I notice something I'd missed the many times before.

Moses was 120 years old, for God's sake. Had he been allowed to go into the Promised Land, what would he have actually encountered? Years of war and conquest, spies, intrigue, and more hardship. I go to the Bible to affirm this fact. Yes, indeed, his scouts did not encounter anything akin to my fantasy of a land overflowing with milk and honey. Rather, their entrance initiated years of struggle and pain. It was the prophetic task of younger leaders to take up where Moses left off, taking up the battles for generations to come.

So what was Moses given in its place? Standing on the mountain overlooking the Promised Land, the Lord said to him, "This is the land which I swore unto Abraham, unto Isaac, and unto Jacob, saying: I will give it unto thy seed." Until the moment of his death, "His eye was not dim, nor his natural force abated." And when he died, "the children of Israel wept for Moses in the plains of Moab for thirty days: so the days of weeping in the mourning for Moses were ended . . .

And there hath not arisen a prophet since in Israel like unto Moses, whom the LORD knew face to face."

Why hadn't I noticed this before? It wasn't a matter of Moses being left to die alone while everybody else got to go to the party. Rather, considering his age and life stage, Moses was actually given a gift far superior to the requirement to fight one more battle. He received, instead, the gift of hope: anticipation of a better future for his progeny. Read beyond one's knee-jerk assumptions about God's punishment, and you'll see that the Bible paints a picture of Moses at the end, not riling against his fate, angry at God, but rather, at peace with his circumstances. When he died, he was mourned, honored, and remembered. This is not a punishment. This is a compassionate gift from a loving God. I could ask no more for myself at the end of my life.

SUMMER

*The meaning of awe
is to realize that life takes place
under wide horizons,
horizons that range beyond
the span of the individual life
or even the life of a nation,
a generation, or an era.*

—Rabbi Abraham Joshua Heschel

67

THE 11TH TRUTH

LUCKY IS ESSENTIAL TO MY VISION OF HOW things can be for me on the wild side of sixty. It helps that with summer finally in full swing, the squirrels are back to their old routines, made all the more poignant by the fact that we are moving away so soon.

Nevertheless, the possibility of a good squirrel to chase is all Lucky needs to feel that life is rich and full. It is impossible to be unhappy when I'm with her. On the way to the park, Lucky is a shameless heart on four legs. She loves the doorman, babies, toddlers, anybody in a wheelchair, appliance delivery people, and traffic cops. She is constantly on the lookout for somebody to greet, and when she sees a candidate, she explodes with joy. When the excitement is past, Lucky relieves herself at the first opportunity. I can only imagine the tales these building corners and fire hydrants are whispering to her. Lucky's ears rise and fall as, with the aplomb of a connoisseur, she adds her own scent to the collective. Without doing anything but pee, she belongs to the whole greater than herself.

Those many who rush by, and yes, the part of me at the other end of the leash who so frequently has more impor- tant things to do, would be well-served to learn from Lucky how little it actually takes to feel that one has found her place in the universe: a place where life is exciting, satisfying, and meaningful. This is not a place one works for, earns, or even deserves. It's something else entirely: a taking in, a savoring, and a participating.

On these occasions, I let the leash go limp, I too admire the squirrel that she has spotted halfway up the tree, and Lucky and I glow contentedly, from the highest hair on the top of my head to the straggliest curl at the tip of her tail. It would not even occur to me to check my BlackBerry for messages. In fact, I have forgotten to bring it along.

Then it suddenly occurs to me. This is another truth of aging that I've learned, not from my mentors in their eighties, not delivered in the midst of a lightning storm, but from my relationship with Lucky. No matter what else is going on in my life, how otherwise inadequate, pressured, worried, or mistaken I may be about transiting to a new life stage, there is always one thing that I can do and that makes it all worthwhile.

Spiritual Truth Number 11: It is purpose enough just to make one dog happy.

68

SPIRITUAL TRAINING

THE IRONY IS THAT WHILE I FEEL MY HEART turning towards the light, the packing boxes stacking up in piles all over the apartment appear to me as headstones in a grave-yard. A stage of my life has ended, but in place of terror, there is a patina of the bittersweet. How can life and death be so deeply engaged in one heart?

I am struck dumb by the answer. While it is true that I am no longer the brand "Carol Orsborn" that once defined my place in the world, I have not entirely left that persona behind. I am the marketer and author. But I am also the infant reaching out to play with the rainbow cast on the wall. The teenager in the embrace of her first kiss. I am graduating from college and attending the graduations of my children. I am being fired for the first time and getting caught in my first lie. I am growing older and needing to put on glasses to read. I am chasing squirrels with Lucky in the park and I am slipping on the ice. I am also what is next to come.

There will be surprises, of this I'm sure. Unexpected joy and unpredictable pleasure. But there are certainties, as well. There will be added pains and lessening abilities. Ultimately, there will be death. Will it be a "good" death—a gentle and loving slipping away into God's embrace? Or will it be difficult and terrifying, like the deaths of so many for whom I have cared?

I have devoted so much of my energy since midlife to hoping to avoid the kind of prolonged, hard aging and death experienced by my parents, viewing the end of life as punishment from an unjust God. I vowed I would do it better, and that such a thing would be under my control.

I remember, too, that I had made a similar vow decades ago, regarding childbirth. I took Lamaze, I learned to breathe, I got my brown belt in karate to learn to toughen up. And still, even while breathing and visualizing and being surrounded by the right music and people and supportive environment, the waves of giving birth engulfed me in uncontrollable pain. I burst the blood vessels in my eyes and screamed for the drugs I had vowed to reject.

Giving birth, facing death: I am being asked once again to deepen my relationship with God. For while it is true that I have forgiven God for barring Moses from the Promised Land, and have declared God just, I have come to realize that my reconciliation was based on a shaky deal. I had come to believe that God had kept Moses out of the Promised Land, but in its place had blessed him with clarity of mind and a peaceful death. But we will not all be so lucky. The bitter truth is that acceptance of aging and mortality is not about learning to negotiate with God to draw from the well only that which we would prefer for ourselves. The spiritual life demands more of us: that we faithfully remove any of the remaining obstacles that separate us from divine love and trust in God, no matter what.

God is not only in the sunshine of our youth, but in the dimming of our minds. God is in the elevation of our patience and compassion, but also in my dad's cold hands still grasping the rail of his hospital bed in the moments after his passing, and in the bruise on Maggie's mother's thigh.

If this is the key, does this information guarantee me that I will do any better in the end than did those who passed before me? After all, I can no longer deny how often I forget where I put the keys. I cannot deny that I experience new, unexpected aches in my joints every day. And if I should succeed at staying alive for twenty or thirty or forty more years, each one of those years hold the potential to accelerate the rate of change and loss.

But what choice is there? To be fully alive, we must take on the task of engaging with the circumstances of our lives—no matter how trivial, awesome, or threatening—without malice, greed, or voluntary ignorance. Rather, we must rise to the challenges that arise moment by moment with courage and understanding. We must become brave enough to tell the truth about pain and joy, life and aging, loss and death. We must become willing to be profoundly transformed. In the words of mystic philosopher Aldous Huxley: "For the lover of God, every moment is a moment of crisis."

69

SKELE-ELF

I KNEW THAT MAGGIE HAD MADE A SAFE RETURN TO Los Angeles, was back with Greg and working at the boutique, because of her posts on Facebook. Her most recent post informed her friends that her mother was doing better, and was going to be moved out of a nursing home and into assisted living. So, it wasn't a complete surprise when Maggie e-mailed to tell me she was going to be back on the East Coast to help her brother with the move. I explained to her that our house was filled with boxes, but that she was welcome to spend the night. In fact, I was thrilled at the prospect, eager to catch up with Maggie's story, hoping it might contain some providential message for me.

The moment she walked through the door, I could tell that things were going much better for Maggie. Her hair was now a hybrid mix of tans, golds, and gray, still spiked, but with the tips blackened as if recently dipped in paint. She looked neither younger than her age, nor older. But rather, her presence made a timeless statement that captured the essence of her unique blend of creativity and beauty. She had managed to tame the unruly parts while keeping the fierce independence. In brief, she had turned herself into a work of art.

We hugged a long time, and then I couldn't help ribbing her.

"I see you've gotten over your aversion to chemicals," I tugged lightly on one of the black-tipped spikes.

"How could I not, given that a chemical saved my marriage."

"Which chemical is that?" I asked.

"Viagra, of course. While I was in Mexico, Greg went to the doctor and got himself a prescription."

"So, your sabbatical from marriage was about the sex?"

"Not really. In fact, not at all. I suppose I just wanted to know that Greg cared enough about me to do something, anything, about me and the marriage. Anyway, after Webster, I finally figured out you don't really need a man to have sex."

Before I could respond, she quickly added: "In fact, you don't need anybody, really, if you get the drift."

"So Webster?"

"Long gone, and so beside the point. The main thing is that my passion is back in full force. In fact, look at this!"

She reached into her bag and pulled out a snapshot of her latest painting. It was her famous elf again, but no longer the symbol of eternal youth. This elf was a skeleton, remarkably approachable despite the fact that it had gone all to bones.

"When did you do this?"

"I sketched this on the plane home from New York. Plus I had a brainstorm. If we turned my studio back into a guesthouse and rented it out, we could make up some of Greg's lost income, and I could cut back to part-time at the boutique."

"But where will you paint?"

"Turns out I'd gone stale working out of that same studio all these years. Time to freshen things up. Watercolors sounded fun. And painting outdoors. So I took the sketch out to Franklin Canyon and set up my easel at the duck pond. Just as I was finishing, some Hollywood guy walked by and asked if he could buy it on the spot. I saw it as a sign and came up with a line of fantasy skeleton figures, angels, fairies, unicorns. I guess it was my way of working out my feelings about aging and mortality as an artist—to stop avoiding or being terrified of it, and to begin making peace with it. You helped me so much when I came to visit, all that talk about acceptance of things, just as they are."

"I'm so happy for you, Maggie. So are you selling your watercolors at the boutique?"

"Kind of. The thing is that something else you said struck me, too—that thing about the buggy whip. To make a long story short, I found a site online that takes images and turns them into coffee mugs, mouse pads, caps, and T-shirts. So, instead of fighting Google images, I'm throwing in with them. Anyway, the Skele-Elf line is going gangbusters at the boutique and online, and Greg's helping out. Turns out he's got a knack for selling things on eBay."

"No more *Twilight Zone?*" I asked.

"He's weaning himself with *Fringe*. Plus, he won't really have the time anymore. One of his friends just found a summer camp for disadvantaged youths that is looking for a volunteer to teach fly-fishing."

70

BONE MOUNTAIN

THE NIGHT MAGGIE LEFT, I HAD A DREAM. The dream started as a nightmare, skeleton elves and bone unicorns chasing me up a mountain in the dark, blood dripping from their fangs. But when I got to the top, everything changed. I looked down into the valley below, and there in the early morning dawn were tens of thousands of people standing there in silence. When I looked more closely, I realized that every one of those people was not only someone I had known in my life, but a skeleton. There was Maggie as well as Maggie's mother. And, too, there were my brother and my mother and father. There was a little girl I recognized to be who I once was, and myself as a teenager and young mother, as well, all skeletons. My old editor Marlene was there, along with the woman at the convention who'd told me her Web site didn't market to Boomer women "because there's no future in it." My children and husband were there and so was Lucky. Tens of thousands of beings, everybody I'd ever known or been, all looking up at me.

Then, at the exact moment the sun reached its zenith, they all started to clap. Thunderous applause as tangible as hugs, telling me I'd done good, welcoming me home.

For what it's worth, I would have preferred if the skeletons had had their skin on. But then again, nobody asked for my opinion. And when all was said and done, skeletons or no, I woke up the next morning feeling strangely affirmed.

71

BEAR ME AWAY

ONE CAN HOPE TO LIVE LONG ENOUGH TO FORGE a consistency between who one is at the deepest levels and one's destiny: that which comes about both because of the previous choices one has made in life, and that which comes to one uninvited.

This is easy enough to imagine on those sunny days, when one is already feeling the embrace of God and the inherent meaning of one's life. I'm sure it was Maggie's upbeat visit that inspired my exuberant dream, for instance. But do we have faith in a relationship with God that will go the distance, when we break denial to contemplate the inevitabilities that positive thinking, alone, cannot forestall?

Pierre Teilhard de Chardin, S. J., has written a poem that leaves no room for exceptions. Here's an excerpt that gets to the heart of the matter.

Bear Me Away

When the signs of age begin to mark my body
(and still more when they touch my mind);
when the ill that is to diminish me or carry me off
strikes from without or is born within me . . .
O God, grant that I may understand that it is you
(provided only my faith is strong enough)
who are painfully parting the fibers of my being
in order to penetrate to the very marrow
of my substance and bear me away within yourself

It is God's grace, and perhaps the truth that undergirds all the rest, that with the challenges, passions, and losses of aging, we are compelled to go deeper. Meaning no longer rests solely in what we recognize now were distractions, entertainments, temporary constructions, and leverage against the inevitable. What new possibilities open for us when we no longer fear the parting of the fibers of our being and trust that it is God who is bearing our losses away?

72

FLASHLIGHT ON

SURROUNDED BY BOXES, WE ONLY KNOW FOR certain what will be our first stop once we leave Brooklyn. We have decided to visit our family in the Smoky Mountains for a while, a reassuring time out with our son, daughter-in-law, and grandson to get our bearings. Then what? We're hoping that one of our many networking e-mails or Dan's scouting trip to Chicago will land on fertile ground and destiny will point the way. We have made a few decisions. We won't consider any opportunities that won't lead us back home to L.A. sooner or later. We can find jobs in L.A., we can work virtually from L.A., and—if nothing materializes—we can retire in L.A.

Retiring would not be my choice. For as I formulate what I'm about to say next, I find that I'm catching myself off-guard. I could not have known one year ago that on this other side of midlife, I would feel so full of life, with so much to give. The wild space, so deep, vast, and threatening for much of this past year, has been miraculously transformed into a promising container of energy. I am curious and excited about the future.

Wasn't it just a few weeks ago that I was slipping on ice,

crawling back into the house as the next generation spun turns around me on their way to work? And just a few days ago when I confronted the painful truth that I am no longer who I once was? Astonishingly, none of the facts of my circumstances have changed. In fact, one could argue that objectively, they've gotten worse. After all, when I began this diary, we had two robust incomes, a penthouse overlooking Manhattan, and a continuity in the storyline of our lives. Now, we're having to tell everybody to forward our mail to our children's address and explain to the car insurance people that we have no permanent residence. But I am back in the full sun of my life. What happened?

Of course, it is so profoundly simple. I had always believed age to be the culmination of the spiritual path. Now I realize how profoundly mistaken I was. It is the beginning.

73

FORTY YEARS

IN THE MIDST OF THE LIGHTNING STORM something profound had shifted for me that continues to deepen and unfold in my heart. While I had not experienced it at the time, I now know that God had been with me through every trial and incident I'd endured, and would continue to be with me through old age and the end of my life, however peaceful or not it may come to pass. And what's more, God will be with me not only through the entirety of my life span, but into the wild space beyond life itself. As my dream of Bone Mountain affirmed, aging and death are neither to be taken as personal failure, nor as something any of us can avoid. Once you've taken the leap of faith that God is with you through it all, there can be no holding back. When it comes to having faith, there is no alternative than to go all in.

Rumi says it best:

Lose Yourself

Lose yourself,
Lose yourself in this love,
you will find everything.

What is your life about, anyway?
nothing but a struggle to be someone,
nothing but a running from your own silence.

As I sit here, writing this now, I am fully aware that it can sometimes feel as if God is asking too much of us. This is especially true when someone we love is suffering, when we ourselves are in the midst of loss, pain, or rejection, or when we contemplate the darker shadows of what the future may have in store for us. But as I learned that night in the lightning storm, there is an antidote. We must let our love of God grow larger than our fear. We must let our love grow so large, our very hearts burst into flame.

74

STORY TIME

CLEARLY, I AM OVER THE EDGE INTO A NEW STAGE OF my life. Some things have been big and dramatic, lightning bolts and messages writ by invisible hand. Others have been subtle but relentless: an exploding fish, a disappointing visit to a spa.

The one thing I am willing to take credit for is this: I've been a faithful witness, recording it all. The 11 Spiritual Truths remind me that something real happened, and I carry them with me everywhere. Of course there continue to be blind spots and imperfections. But there are also patches of growing awareness. In fact, these are usually the spots that hurt the most.

The thing is that turning your attention towards the pain doesn't make you feel any better. But as I learned not only from my own struggles, but from Maggie's, as well, your very willingness to feel everything, including uncomfortable emotions, is the only way to undercut the temptation to come to superficial resolution. It takes a different kind of courage to be able to encounter pain without needing to fix or do anything about it. And it is this willingness to endure that turns out to be the cutting edge of spiritual growth.

Meanwhile, my own cycle of life—the alternating waves of wisdom and pain—continue to lap against the shore of my consciousness, leaving behind the effluence of, if not perfect, growing awareness. There are luminescent seashells, but too, there are rotting fish. So this is what Connie meant when she said we are not simply growing old, we are growing whole. Polished glass and bug-eaten seaweed. Not just standing full-faced with our noses turned toward the sun. But at the same exact time, our ankles sinking deeper into the mud.

Sometimes God whispers, sometimes God shouts, and sometimes God is silent. The key is to recognize that you are in a transition into a new stage of life, and that the one thing that is up to you is whether you will make getting old a tragedy, or embark upon it as another of life's great adventures.

When you remember to trust God, you are equipped to live every day to the fullest, to love the ordinary, and to take life as it arises.

75

OUR LAST WALK IN BROOKLYN

WE'VE GOT TIME FOR ONE LAST WALK ON BEDFORD before the move. The walk down the avenue feels especially precious, set against the blur of young people rushing past us towards the subway. On weekends, when we have Lucky with us, they will at least occasionally stop and reach down to pet her, acknowledging the old people on the other end of the leash just long enough to ask us her name. But today, a workday, we are invisible as they hurry past, seeing nothing but the Metro-Card passes in their hands.

Lucky pauses at the stairwell to the subway, down which we have watched Dan descend a hundred times. We urge her against instinct to move with us past the stop. At first she is confused, forced against her will to break old habits. But before long, she realizes that there are fresh, unexplored garbage cans just ahead and as always, the possibility of yet another squirrel.

Venturing as we are through wild space, I do not stride into the unknown with the bravado of youth. Rather, I am feeling slow and old. But this does not seem like a bad thing. As the young people disappear into the subway and into the heat of their lives, I am struck with the awareness that the portion of the journey that lies ahead for me is not one of mastery. I have already explored the outer edges of achievement born of drive and willpower. Just as I played Scheherazade to my mother's hunger for story, so have I passed many decades earning my keep being clever, opinioned, insightful, and forceful.

To stop "doing" my personality and leave space for God requires making the shift from pushing to make things happen to being present to opportunities beyond my imagination, expectation, and control. And in the literal and metaphysical space this has opened up, gentle waves of illumination have resumed lapping at my feet. Heaven embraces Dan, Lucky, and me with the sudden, unexpected sense that all is well and enough.

76

THE ALTAR

ODDLY ENOUGH, THE LAST BOX TO HAVE BEEN unpacked after our arrival in New York is now the last waiting to be repacked. It's the altar table, cleared at last of the yellow pads and calculators, and lovingly restored to its intended state. The sacred texts are there, as is the prayer shawl, the incense, and the notebook "Carol's Prayers," still blank. I have spent so much of this year seated before the altar, attempting to crack through my resistance, I was unprepared for what happened next.

I wanted to pray. And I knew exactly what it was I would be asking for. I took up the pen and began writing.

77

READY TO MOVE

AS DAN BEGAN PACKING THE ALTAR TABLE ITEMS around me, I sat there, scribbling madly into the notebook. After that first long-awaited prayer, prayer after prayer flowed out of me until thirty pages had been filled.

Gently reminding me that the moving people would be here sometime between one and four, Dan let me continue writing, packing up everything but the notebook itself. The last thing to go was the prayer shawl from around my shoulders. Finally, it was time to leave.

The car had been stuffed with everything we need to get us through the next six months in transit. Everything else is going into storage. Our first stop will be the Smoky Mountains, where our son's family eagerly awaits us, and eventually, we dream about ending up back in our little cottage in Los Angeles, hopefully before winter sets in. Maggie is thrilled, and so are the neighborhood dogs. We think it will be fun to drive Route 66 and stop along the way in New Mexico, Las Vegas, and Big Bear Lake. Everything else is in flux.

Well, not everything. Our faith is holding steady. So is our love. Our sense of adventure is intact and so is our curiosity. We have Lucky and we have each other. We are ready for what is next, knowing that we have everything we need for the one thing that is still in our power to guarantee, even on the wild side of sixty: the best outcome possible.

78

TURNING TOWARD THE FUTURE

I REMEMBER A TIME, NOT LONG AGO, WHEN I thought I was calling the shots in my life . . . a time when I thought I knew how to protect the vulnerable places. But on this side of midlife, I know now that things sometimes spin out of control, emptying out certainty and leaving us tender, exposed. But I've also learned something else, along the way. The essence that was captured in the first of the 11 Spiritual Truths: the less of whom we think we used to be, the more room there is for God.

As we turn towards the future, I can appreciate that I no longer view being old as an ending to my involvement in life in a vital way. Rather, I see it as the initiation of a new life stage during which I am more empowered than ever to achieve my true human potential. This is what aging now means to me: the throwing off of knee-jerk responses to the impositions of others and the reclamation of the fullness of life that I now see as my God-given right.

I have spent a long year chasing God and squirrels in Brooklyn, learning the lessons and getting my first taste of what it means to be fully alive. Now I am at last able to celebrate the culmination of all of my accomplishments, everything that has happened this year, and all the many decades of my life that have brought me to this time and this place.

I am old and I am free. And for this, I give thanks.

CAROL'S PRAYER

God,

In the past, I have come to you
asking for safety and comfort.

But today, I ask only for you to be with
me as I plunge over the edge and into
the mystery.

I am grateful to you, God, for the gift
of growing old and for the promise of a
future that is always free and full of
possibilities.

Amen

P.S. God bless the squirrels.

APPENDICES

The 11 Spiritual Truths of Aging

1. The less of whom we think we used to be, the more room there is for God.

2. Others' rejection is our freedom.

3. When we are doing God's work, we are not the judge of our success.

4. Regret is God calling us to forgive more and love with fewer conditions.

5. We can dance with rather than struggle against the essence of who we are.

6. The gift of longevity provides ample opportunity to not only grow old, but to grow whole.

7. When confronted with ultimate concerns, we can be more curious than afraid.

8. We have never been better equipped than we are now to face life as it arises.

9. Ultimately, hope is more important than peace.

10. We don't always get to take a leap of faith. Sometimes, we are pushed.

11. It is purpose enough to just make one dog happy.

Q&A WITH THE AUTHOR

1. Why do you call your work *Fierce with Age* rather than *Serene with Age?*

Serenity is something for which we all strive. But the mystics of many traditions have a broader understanding of what it means to walk the spiritual path. Most conceptions of spiritual development equate spiritual progress with letting go of the illusion of control and putting our faith into a power greater than ourselves.

Of course, most of us prefer the notion that we are calling the shots in our lives, applying ourselves to making things turn out the way we want, and feeling that we have mastery over our circumstances. But, the daunting part about aging is this: some and eventually all of our old tricks no longer work. We realize how much of our sense of mastery over our fates had always been limited, at best. At last, we are forced to loosen up our grip on the wheel of our lives, and led to confront our fears.

This psychologically and spiritually healthy vision of aging does not always look like serenity. While we may be quiet and peaceful sometimes, we may be rabble-rousing and making trouble at other times. Sometimes we are faced with external challenges, such as job loss or illness. Other times our challenges are internal: anxiety about the future, for instance, or feelings of personal failure. The truth is, as long as we keep growing through life, there will be anxious moments, regrets, and self-doubt. But there will be transiting, transforming, and overcoming, too.

We may prefer serenity, but the attributes that allow us to break denial, shattering the impositions and fantasies, can best be described as "fierce."

2. What is the link between spirituality and consciousness?

At midlife and beyond, it is no accident that we increasingly ask questions about meaning and purpose. These are, at heart, spiritual questions—defined in the broadest possible terms. The truth is that aging brings with it both gains and losses. We may hope to experience broader perspectives and increased wisdom, but we also find ourselves to be increasingly staring mortality in the eye.

Those who deny or romanticize the shadow side of aging are broadsided and ill-prepared to handle life as it arises. In identifying with mainstream society's aversion toward aging, they become part of the suppression of what in other eras and societies has been embraced as an organic part of the life cycle with a value and meaning of its own. Embracing aging, however, means being willing to ask questions of ultimate concern. We are forced to deepen ourselves spiritually, or at the very least, philosophically. This takes a genuine maturity of spirit, a new stage of growth that many in our generation of Boomers have been preparing for all of our lives.

3. I'm over sixty and I don't feel old. Why do you?

When I first realized that I was suddenly feeling old, I viewed this as a bad thing. I was very enmeshed in the stereotypes of aging that contemporary Western society holds and felt embarrassed and ashamed that I was feeling "old" at the same age that others were still running companies and climbing the Himalayas. The truth is that I didn't have any conscious control over the circumstances—internal or external—that pushed me over to the wild space beyond midlife. Gerontologists identify three stages of being old, and I was situated developmentally and chronologically in the stage they refer to as "young old" (ages 60-69). The middle stage of old is referred to as "old old" (ages 70-79) and the third stage is "oldest-old" (80-plus). But feeling old is not necessarily related to any particular age.

More to the point, as the year unfolded, most if not all the negative connotations of being old dropped away. I stopped seeing age only as illness and imposition, and began seeing it as increased freedom and activation of new, unprecedented levels of self-affirmation and spiritual growth.

4. You've spent your entire adult life writing spiritual books. Why weren't you better prepared spiritually for aging?

In retrospect, God has been with me from the beginning of my life, through every life stage. I have not always been aware of God's presence, and admit that I have sometimes done quite a bit to block, ignore, or deny God's grace at work in my life. It helps to use the image of the spiral to describe how it is that it can sometimes appear I'm going in exactly the wrong direction—slipping down the backside of the spiral—only to learn from what I've endured to find myself sooner (or sometimes later) back on the upswing, reaching new heights of awareness and intimacy with the divine. This convergence at the peak of each spiral can last anywhere from a moment to months.

While I sometimes forget when I'm on the downward swing, I do believe that everything that occurs furthers my progress and that God is in every twist and turn. Obviously, I wrote much of this diary on the downswing. When I began, I wasn't thinking about God very much at all, and when I did, I was mostly angry. During the process of keeping a diary over this year's period, I was able to revisit some of my favorite authors, as well as some of my previous "precocious" writings, seeing new facets of both their and my own spiritual lives, and our respective relationships to God.

5. What is your most important takeaway about getting old from this year?

That old is not synonymous with hopelessness, marginalization, or abandonment. There is nothing inherent in becoming old—including illness and loss—that calls for the solicitation of shame or embarrassment. In fact, if one feels old and allows any of the above negative emotions to dominate the experience, it is—in truth—a call to action.

Through a combination of psycho-spiritual work, spontaneous growth, and grace, you can come to experience a level of freedom that can't be shaken because it is not dependent on the affirmation of others. Benefiting from a lifetime of trial and error, you will be better equipped now than during any previous stage in your life to handle whatever comes your way.

But if you are only looking for peace and comfort, you will be missing your opportunity. This is the time in your life to embrace the greater span of the human potential and to become whole.

6. I'm sad about the passing of my youth. Is it okay to mourn?

Of course, being sad, being authentic is part of what it means to be whole. In fact, the passing away of any life stage is a loss, as well as a gain. Don't deny yourself the full range of emotions—just don't get stuck in the negative end of the spectrum simply because you've unconsciously bought into the stereotypes.

7. Have you gotten over your ennui with narrative?

Apparently.

AN INVITATION TO STAY CONNECTED

Waiting for visitors at www.FierceWithAge.com, The Online Digest of Boomer Wisdom, Inspiration, and Spirituality:

- Downloadable free eBook: *Carol's Prayers: The Fierce with Age Companion for Spirituality and Aging,* including the 30 prayers that flowed out of Carol at the end of her year in Brooklyn.

- Free reader's and discussion guides for book club members.

- Bi-weekly summaries and daily updates of the best writing about spirituality and aging on the Web.

- Carol's print and video blog along with the opportunity to join in the conversation with others who are Fierce with Age.

Engage with the Fierce with Age Facebook community by "Liking" our page:

http://www.facebook.com/FierceWithAge

Follow Dr. Carol Orsborn on Twitter:

@CarolOrsborn

For Dr. Carol Orsborn's speeches, brand blogging, and marketing counsel:

www.CarolOrsbornPhD.com

If you would like to contact Carol Orsborn directly, the e-mail address for Fierce with Age is:

Carol@FierceWithAge.com

THE FIERCE WITH AGE ONLINE RETREAT

Let's Become Fierce with Age Together: Passing beyond midlife initiates a new life stage, bearing with it high anticipation, celebration, and sometimes, outright terror. If you are determined to make the next stage of your life as vital as the decades that have come before, join Dr. Carol Orsborn for this interactive, self-paced spiritual retreat.

WHAT YOU RECEIVE

The Core Retreat: You will receive a spiritual lesson, exercise, meditation, or contemplative reading every weekday for three weeks, delivered to your inbox directly from Dr. Orsborn. You decide how, when, and to what depth to follow the prompts.

The Enhanced Retreat: You will receive all of the above plus two 50-minute one-on-one counseling sessions with Dr. Orsborn by phone or Skype.

BENEFITS:

- Initiate a new level of freedom not dependent on the affirmation of others

- Replace the stereotypes of aging with the embrace of a new, vital life stage

- Let go of who you once were to re-energize your vision of who you are becoming

- Build an inspired plan for the future including your aspirations, relationships, practical decisions, and well-being

- Clarify your relationship to spirituality and religion

- Explore the key issues surrounding the ultimate concerns everyone who hopes to become fierce with age must address

"The retreat led me face-to-face with the unequivocal fact that my faith and spirituality is what will gracefully carry me through the full life journey and beyond."

—Kathy Sporre, director of the Fergus Falls Senior Citizens Program, Inc., and champion of the International Council on Active Aging's "Changing the Way We Age®" Campaign

"Dr. Carol Orsborn is a gifted guide into the shadow side of aging. Her virtual retreat awakened the possibility of overcoming fears to make way for new awareness, hope, even freedom."

—Phyllis Goldberg, Ph.D., consultant in family dynamics, www.HerMentorCenter.com

EACH WEEK OF THE RETREAT HAS A DIFFERENT FOCUS

Week One: The topic is breaking denial and re-visioning aging from a deeper, more spiritual perspective for yourself.

The questions/topics include:

- Appreciating your questions and concerns not as problems to be solved, but as the heart of the spiritual journey.

- Setting an intention worthy of you: to what are you being called?

- What are your spiritual strengths and weaknesses? Take inventory of your progress towards spiritual maturity in the areas of preparation for the future, your ambition, love and relationships including parenting grown children, beauty, health, purpose and meaning, and coming to terms with loss and mortality.

- What is a psychologically and spiritually healthy vision of aging? Explore how you can avoid tending towards either romanticizing or reviling growing older.

- How will your personal spiritual and religious history translate into the future? Discover in what ways you have been in denial, and to what awarenesses you are awakening.

Week Two: The topic is taking a deep dive into your heart to construct a blueprint for this new stage of your life that is guaranteed to deliver on its promise.

- What qualities did you neglect in the first half of your life that you are now free to develop? Let go of who you once were to re-energize your vision of who you are becoming.

- Build an inspired plan for the future including your aspirations, relationships, practical decisions, and well-being.

- Learn to solve problems and make decisions by receiving rather than doing.

- Discover the importance of discernment: which voices are worthy of your trust, both external and internal? How do you know when it's God who is calling you?

- Once you know what you want your life to be like decades from now, what should you be doing ten years, five years, one year, six months, one month, and one week from now? And most important, what should you be doing next?

Week Three: The topic is addressing your ultimate concerns regarding aging, loss, and mortality in order to find freedom and peace.

- What does it mean to be free—especially when thinking about facing physical and cognitive losses, connections to those for whom you care, the erosion of social status, and ultimately life itself? Identify in what ways you have already let go as well as where you are still holding on.

- In what ways can regret, shame, guilt, and fear be given a constructive role to play? Heal your unfinished business and discover that you are not only growing older, you are growing whole.

- Explore how the dynamic tension between accepting marginalization and fighting against it is playing out in your life. See how the stereo-types of aging are subtly holding you back from fulfilling your true human potential.

- What is a spiritually/psychologically healthy response to those times when we feel God has deserted us? Face and address your greatest fears and concerns by going deeper.

- Celebrate the many ways in which growing older is enabling you to become more fully yourself.

Sign Up at www.FiercewithAge.com

SOURCES

BOOKS BY CAROL ORSBORN

The Art of Resilience: 100 Paths to Wisdom and Strength in an Uncertain World. New York: Three Rivers Press/Random House, 1997.

Vibrant Nation: What Women 50+ Know, Think, Do and Buy. With Stephen Reily. Louisville: VN Books, 2010.

The Year I Saved My (downsized) Soul: A Boomer Woman's Search for Meaning ... and a Job. Louisville: Vibrant Nation Books, 2009.

Boom: Marketing to the Ultimate Power Consumer—the Baby Boomer Woman. With Mary Brown. New York: Amacom Publishing, 2006.

How Would Confucius Ask for a Raise? New York: William Morrow, 1993 and New York: Avon Books, 1994.

Inner Excellence: A Book About Meaning, Spirit and Success. New York: Amacom Publishing, 1999.

"Integrity in Business," in *The Soul of Business,* Ed. Charles Garfield. New York: Hay House, 1997.

Nothing Left Unsaid: Words to Help You and Your Loved Ones Through the Hardest Times. Berkeley, California: Conari Press, 2001.

The Silver Pearl: Our Generation's Journey to Wisdom. With Dr. Jimmy Laura Smull. Chicago: Ampersand, Inc. 2005.

Solved by Sunset: The Self-Guided Intuitive Decision-Making Retreat. New York: Harmony/Random House, 1996 and New York: Crown, 1997.

Speak the Language of Healing: Living with Breast Cancer without Going to War. Foreword by Jean Shinoda Bolen, M.D. With Susan Kuner et al. Berkeley, California: Conari Press, 1997.

SOURCES BY OTHERS REFERENCED IN AND/OR INFLUENCING THIS MEMOIR:

Aging Well. Vaillant, George E., M.D. New York: Little, Brown and Company, 2002.

Second Chance. Barrett, Marvin. New York: Parabola Books, 1999.

The Five Stages of Soul: Charting the Spiritual Passages that Shape our Lives. Moody, Harry R. and Carroll, David. New York: Anchor Books, 1998.

The Fountain of Age. Friedan, Betty. New York: Touchstone Books, 1993.

From Age-ing to Sage-ing. Schachter-Shalomi, Zalman. New York: Warner Books, 1997.

The Essential Rumi. Rumi; Barks, Coleman, trans. San Francisco, California: HarperCollins, 1995.

The Gift of Years: Growing Old Gracefully. Chittister, Joan. New York: BlueBridge, 2008.

A Guide to the Spiritual Dimension of Care for People with Alzheimer's Disease and Related Dementia: More than Body, Brain and Breath. Shamy, Eileen. London and Philadelphia: Jessica Kingsley Publishers, 1997.

The Holy Scriptures. Philadelphia: The Jewish Publication Society of America, 1917.

Hymns to an Unknown God: Awakening the Spirit in Everyday Life. Keen, Sam. New York: Bantam Books, 1994.

The I Ching. Wilhelm, Richard, and Baynes, Cary F. Foreword by Carl Jung. Princeton, New Jersey: Princeton University Press, 1950.

Journal of a Solitude. Sarton, May. New York: W. W. Norton, 1973.

Magic of the Ordinary. Winkler, Gershon. Berkeley, CA: North Atlantic Books, 2003.

Man's Search for Meaning. Frankl, Viktor. Boston: Beacon Press, 1962.

The Measure of My Days. Scott-Maxwell, Florida. New York: Knopf, 1968.

The New Oxford Annotated Bible. Metzger, Bruce M., and Murphy, Roland E., eds. New York: Oxford University Press, 1991.

No Act of Love Is Ever Wasted: The Spirituality of Caring for Persons with Dementia. Thibault, Jane Marie and Morgan, Richard L. Nashville: Upper Room Books, 2009.

A Passion for Truth. Heschel, Abraham Joshua. New York: Ferrar, Straus and Giroux, 1973.

Scarred by Struggle, Transformed by Hope. Chittister, Joan. Grand Rapids, Michigan: William B. Eerdmans, 2003.

Staring at the Sun: Overcoming the Terror of Death. Yalom, Irvin D. San Francisco, California: Josey-Bass, 2008.

Who Am I . . . Now That I'm Not Who I Was? Conversations with Women in Mid-life and the Years Beyond. Goldman, Connie. Minneapolis: Nodin Press, 2009.

ABOUT THE AUTHOR

CAROL ORSBORN, PH.D., IS FOUNDER OF FIERCE WITH AGE, the Online Digest of Boomer Wisdom, Inspiration and Spirituality. She is an internationally recognized thought leader on the Boomer generation. Through her retreats, blogs, speeches, marketing consulting, and over twenty books, Carol has chronicled the challenges her generation has faced and the stereotypes they've defied as they've transited from early parenthood through midlife crisis and beyond.

Carol has been a leading voice for her generation of women since she founded Overachievers Anonymous in the late 1980s, credited as a progenitor of both the simplicity and work/life balance movements. Since then, she has appeared multiple times on the *Today* show, *Oprah, NBC Nightly News,* and in the pages of *The New York Times* and *USA Today.* Carol is currently a blogger with *Huffington Post, Beliefnet,* and *Next Avenue,* PBS's initiative for the Boomer generation. In addition to her leadership role with Fierce with Age, Carol is Executive Director of CoroFaith, offering audio-based spiritual content to hospitals and the aging community. Previously, she served as co-founder of FH Boom, the first global initiative by a top ten PR company dedicated to helping brands connect with the Boomer generation.

Carol, a Phi Beta Kappa graduate of UC Berkeley, received her Masters of Theological Studies and Doctorate in the History and Critical Theory of Religion from Vanderbilt University, specializing in adult development and ritual studies. She has done postgraduate work in spiritual guidance at both Stillpoint and the Spirituality Center at Mount St. Mary's College in Los Angeles and the New Seminary of Interfaith Studies in Manhattan.

Dr. Orsborn continues life on the wild side of midlife at the side of her husband Dan, and their dog, Lucky, splitting their time between Los Angeles, California, and Nashville, Tennessee. She is the mother of two adult children, and the grandmother of one.

Printed in the USA
CPSIA information can be obtained
at www.ICGtesting.com
JSHW082159140824
68134JS00014B/323